A WORLD OF DIFFERENCE

- Future Voices
Edited by Justine Horne

 Young**Writers**

First published in Great Britain in 2008 by:
Young Writers
Remus House
Coltsfoot Drive
Peterborough
PE2 9JX
Telephone: 01733 890066
Website: www.youngwriters.co.uk

SB ISBN 978-1 84431 786 8

Foreword

Young Writers' Big Green Poetry Machine is a showcase for our nation's most brilliant young poets to share their thoughts, hopes and fears for the planet they call home.

Young Writers was established in 1991 to nurture creativity in our children and young adults, to give them an interest in poetry and an outlet to express themselves. Seeing their work in print will encourage them to keep writing as they grow, and become our poets of tomorrow.

Selecting the poems has been challenging and immensely rewarding. The effort and imagination invested by these young writers makes their poems a pleasure to enjoy reading time and time again.

Contents

Stephanie Bean (12)	25
Chris Wilson (12)	25
Jessica Williams (12)	26
Jamie Boyle (12)	26
Natasha Flinn (12)	27

Frodsham College, Frodsham

Emma Jones (12)	27
Elliott Prendergast (13)	27
Emily Davies (12)	28
Eloise Edwards (13)	28
Lucy Wallbank (13)	29
Neena Tamber (12)	29

Guilsborough School, Guilsborough

Forest Onderka-Lang (14)	30
Sophie Humphries (13)	30

Hall Green Secondary School, Hall Green

Leena Sharma (13)	31
Suhayl Iqbal (13)	32

Kirkby College, Kirkby-in-Ashfield

Amy Musgrave (14)	33
Megan Abrahall (14)	33
Ailish Dalton-Winfield (14)	34
Adam Gage (13)	34
Dean Kennedy (14)	35
Melissa Tyler (14)	35
Alice Warren (14)	36
Jessica Playford (12)	36
Patricia Hartley (13)	37
Bethany Atkin (12)	37
Tia Elvidge (13)	38
Bethany Osborne (12)	38
Demi-Jay Lound (12)	39
Lucy Stendall (14)	39
Shannon Owens (12)	40
Billy Beaver (12)	41

Neston High School, Neston

Sophie Pitchford (12)	41
Rebecca Washington (14)	41
Peter Ankcorn (11)	42
Connor Jellicoe (12)	42
Charlie Rattenshaw (13)	43
Dean Norman (12)	43
Jake Carr (13)	43
Ben Everitt (13)	44
Katie Nall (14)	44
Catherine Gould (13)	45
Casper Evans (12)	45
Matthew Lewis (13)	45
Kelly Cubbins (13)	46
Dominic Benson (13)	46
Chloe Leadbetter (13)	46
Harry Smith (12)	47
Ben Brothwell (12)	47
Mollie Simmons (13)	47
Sophie Roscoe (12)	48
Ben Stott (12)	49
Ryan Traill (14)	50
Elliot Banton (13)	50
Alice Evans (13)	51
Chris Jones (12)	51
Joshua Cooke (12)	51
Edward Williams (12)	52
Wesley Osunjimi (12)	52
Ellie Jones (12)	53
Grace Johnson (13)	53
Georgia Macey (13)	53
Matthew Davies (13)	54
Jonathan Lee (13)	54
Jack Daker (13)	55
Andrew Adams (13)	55
John Collins (13)	56
Emily Egner (13)	56
Catherine Williams (13)	57
Sophie Toll (13)	57
Daniel Foulkes (13)	58

Sean Colley (13)	58
Alicia Webb (13)	59
Jenni Potter (13)	59
Ashley Davies (13)	60
Aimee Thompson (13)	60
Laura McGrath (12)	61
Tara Hatton (13)	61
Jaimie Sadler (12)	62
Matthew Rigby (12)	62
Eleanor Newall (13)	63
April Plant (13)	63
Sarah Ellis (13)	64

Ridgeway High School, Prenton
Lauren Hawksford (14)	64
Stephanie Cragg (11)	65
Keiran Stanley (14)	65
Charlie Evans (12)	66
Daniel Nall (12)	66
Amy Griffiths (14)	67
Becky Simpson (12)	68
Dale Longmuir (13)	69
Hannah McLaughlin (13)	69
Dayle Jones (14)	70
Alexandria Steele (12)	70
Katie Rutter (12)	71
Jake Lilliott (13)	71

Sandbach High School & Sixth Form College, Sandbach
Hannah Carter-Bloor (12)	72
Megan Holden (11)	73
Isobel Harrop (11)	74
Georgina Innocent-Galletley (11)	74
Jessica Cronshaw (15)	75
Stephanie Lea (12)	76
Rachel Biddle (12)	77
Stephanie Bell (12)	78
Holly Williams (12)	78
Becksy Olpin (12)	79
Charlotte Halliday	80
Grace Jeffs (12)	81

Kristin Gilmore (12)	82
Lydia Sourbutts (12)	83
Lucy Furber (12)	84
Ellie Doubleday (12)	85
Bethany Phillips (12)	86
Hannah Beckett	87
Rebecca Hewitt (12)	88

The Duston School, Northampton

Amita Khera (12)	88
Grace Tredré (12)	89
Terri-Ann Greatorex (11)	89
Lloyd Butcher (14)	90
Thomas Rust (11)	90
Chloe Hunter (12)	91
Melissa Sibley (13)	91
Melissa Barnard (11)	92
David Whitehead (12)	92
Jack Kushniruk (12)	93
Aleshia Cannell (12)	93
Joe Burrows (12)	94
Emily Bustin (13)	94
Maddison Jones (13)	95
Daniel Dyer (11)	95
Laura Leyman (15)	96
Tom Harrison (15)	96
Jamie Kelly (11)	97
Liam Tuck (15) & Abdul Kalam (14)	97
Becky French-Wade (15)	97
Perry Burford (12)	98
Rosie Worster (15)	98
Emily Liddle (15)	99

The Meden School & Technology College, Warsop

Holly Smith & Katie Thomas (12)	99
Rebecca Fretwell (12)	100
Matthew Simpson (12)	100
Leigh Hearnshaw (12)	101
Troy Davies (13)	102

The National School, Hucknall

Tuxford School, Tuxford

The Poems

The Big Green Poetry Machine

The Big Green Poetry Machine
What a strange name that seems
What on Earth can I write,
That will suit that name right?

A chant to stop a natural disaster?
A poem about the icebergs melting faster?
A song that prevents forest burnings?
Why do humans have these yearnings?

Why do we want more coal?
Or need to visit the North Pole?
Do we need that much electricity?
Live with more simplicity . . .

Why can we not be pleased,
With the lot we have received?

We are speeding up global warming,
With lots of new deserts forming.
There is a lot that we can do
If we don't want to go that way too.

We can start off with recycling
And do a bit of bicycling
Stop riding out in cars
And not leaving things on charge
Turn your TV off standby
Cut down your water supply.

These little things and more
Are all it takes to
Stop
The
World
Breaking
Up
Completely.

Felicia C J Gatenby (16)

It Makes No Sense To Me

Africa's a country
that cannot be erased
they're unlucky enough
to live in poverty.

No food
no clean water
I dread to think how they feel
dirty and unfree

No cleanliness
no life for me
disease and death
spreads like fire

Across that wasteland
they call Africa
Africa has a history
that cannot be erased

Poverty's no one
it kills and depresses
families get separated
they get orphaned and lonely

Poverty's no one
well it's not to me.

Tanisha Plows (13)

My Generation Poem

Generations pass, generations change
Even more clichés, even more strange
Too much judgment, too much face
Automatic grouping of the human race
Not knowing the person inside, that's the only flaw
You need to see past the Converse and the G-Star Raw

Worrying about everything even life itself
Trying to make the most of life on the shelf
Hanging out with friends, having late nights
Rioting around school, towards rumoured fights
Supporting Sheffield Wednesday or Sheffield United
Forever falling in love, however unrequited

Live young and live loud
Always stand out from the crowd
Sat on MSN, till 3 in the morning
Walking to school, freezing cold and yawning
Thinking you're cool, chewing chuddy in class
Until your best mate puts his hand up to grass

But some aren't like that, they prefer to hide
Because they're confused and angry inside
Many reasons, maybe even the loss of a loved one
All that *they* know is something is gone
But things do get better, it's a definite rule
Even if they have tons of homework from school

So if you feel like your problems are bursting the seams
Remember, life isn't as bad as it seems
Live life to the full, be who you want to be
Do just those two things and you'll come to see
That it's best to make the most of every day
Because just yet, you don't know who you are anyway.

Ruby Lee (14)

Bang

Get up, get dressed, it's another day
I gotta sell the grass, just to get my pay
No life, no job, nothing at all
Just another hood rat, looking strong and tall.

Hood up, trainers on, Rolex from my last theft
He retaliated, all turned into death
I prayed to God for forgiveness, no reply
He's looking down on me thinking waster, thief, too sly.

I'm out of my door now, hood up, looking dead
Be fast, look sharp, try to avoid Feds
First custom 5 grams and it's all good
Smoke the weed, get high, find some more bud.

Last custom, 5 fears on the day
Gotta load of weed, gonna get a load of pay
Hold on a minute though, one's pulling out a gun
I gotta run, before my time's finished, over, done.

Bang, bang, go the bullets, vibrating in my head
Time's up, life finished, now I am stone cold dead
I wish I had a life, go to school, do well,
But instead I am on the verge of going to hell.

Get up, get dressed, it's another day
Am 13 with a mother, who is on drugs; cocaine
But all's over and I'm burning in the fires of hell
Bang, that could have changed, if I did well.

Sharmilla Fearon (14)
Bigwood School, Warren Hill

War

War damages our eco-systems,
War kills our brothers and sisters,
Animals have to run away.
Because of war they cannot stay,
Zebras, seals, dads, mums,
All of these have homes to run.

War damages our eco-systems
War kills our brothers and sisters,
Pandas will have no bamboo,
Killing animals we shall not do,
Wildlife, plants and humans too,
Stop the war!
And now I'm through.

Abigail Roddis (13)
Bigwood School, Warren Hill

No Reason

Why carry a knife?
Protection?
Is it cool?

How is killing cool?
How is killing protecting?

Knives kill
No word of a lie
What good can it do if it makes people die?
People with family
People with friends
People with people
The list never ends

So save yourself, save us all
Leave the knife.
Alone.

Joe Hicks (14)
Bigwood School, Warren Hill

A Normal Day Has Begun
(For the people who died I survived Hiroshima)

A normal day has begun,
The sky so blue and the sun,
A normal morning is here,
But that's what we both think my dear.

What I say is a true tale
A blinding light, a shockwave,
Cars tip over and trains derail,
Were we brave or stupid not to give into this war?
This powerful bomb swept away homes and lives it tore.

Hiroshima town, a peaceful place,
Our city was about to be erased.
Hiroshima town, so sweet,
Even birds had a peaceful tweet.

The bomb plummeted down towards our families and friends,
I swear to you this is not pretend
A roaring explosion ripped through my body, then a massive fireball
appeared, followed by a mushroom cloud.
People were vaporised, people were injured.

A lot of people died
Men, women, children, even babies were affected badly,
Most of them lost their lives so sadly,
Many had cuts, many had burns, but most didn't survive,
I swear to God I am so lucky to be alive.

A roar of a bomber engine has come,
For this war were we to blame?
Our people, our innocent people,
Paid dearly for our government's mistakes.

An atomic bomb called Little Boy
Please listen to me when I say it's not a toy,
It claimed over 100,000 lives that day
Innocent people killed by the *USA*.

So not everyone is as lucky as me and you,
Just think what us survivors have been through,
Put these murderous weapons away,
The bomb sent by the USA,

Lock them away, never let them come out,
It's never been what life is about,
So look at these lives bombs take away,
Our innocent people killed by the USA.

Shannon Munks (14)
Bigwood School, Warren Hill

Pain, Shame And Blame

Sat in the streets gazing at the wealthy pockets of passers-by.
Stretching out a hand wishing for someone to take it and sing
                                                as you cry.
What brought them to this very pain?
Lost souls of wanderers floating in the Dead Sea.
Waiting for help or someone who cares to see.
What brought them to this very shame?
Illusions in the distance of shelter, water and food.
Trembling in the gritty Earth as watchers laugh, a change of mood.
How to free yourself from blame?
Give them shelter, give them heat.
Change their clothes let them eat.
We stand as one, we stand as all.
The stronger we are the less we will fall.
So call to your neighbour with smiles and laughter.
As if we don't, it won't be a happily ever after.
Don't give to receive, give for the glory.
What was pain before, is now joy from the heavens.
So make that change, for your sins will be forgiven.

Sharice Chambers (14)
Bigwood School, Warren Hill

A Perfect World?

Would you call this a perfect world?
Well let the truth be uncurled,
People live to see others in horror and fear,
To think their own problems will disappear.

Is it a perfect place for living?
Is there anything left to believe in?
The innocent murdered because of their culture,
Spied on by enemies like a vulture.

Are we the perfect residents,
Living by the rules of the confused presidents,
Living for racism,
Poverty and war?
This world could be worth so much more.

Can this be the perfect life?
When all that is natural, the wildlife is being destroyed for our own
needs.
Will it be us or the world that concedes?

Ashleigh Perkins (14)
Bigwood School, Warren Hill

War

Bang, bang. My friend is dead
Everyone around me is dead.
Falling to the ground, falling to their grave
They must be brave.
Falling, falling to the ground,
Now I am dead.
All the pain, all the dread,
In my head there is so much,
All I need is a bullet to the head.

Dale Lowe (12)
Bigwood School, Warren Hill

War

When two worlds collide, crashing and smashing like an angry sea,
Haunting your mind with ghostly images,
With cries from friends and soldiers repeating endlessly in your head,
Like a record player on loop.

This place is: lonely, forbidding, tragic.
The past was quiet, the future is loud.
As smiles merge into frowns the clouds drip from the dirty green sky.
It reminds me of how different this world is.

A bomb arrives close at my foot,
As I feel my time is up, I close my eyes.
The sweet scent of my wife's cooking, roast chicken and brownies,
As the white light comes closer and closer, I relax and look ahead.
. . . What will happen to me?

Stephen Landon (14)
Bigwood School, Warren Hill

The Destruction Of Me

The hurricane comes our way.
Not again I say
A lot of devastation in a day.
Rescue services kept at bay
I fell sleeping on hay.
But in fact I'm sleeping on clay.

Thunderstorms come at last.
Causing a mighty blast.
The mass of an outbreak.
We're left in its wake.
To quiver and shake.

Here comes a tsunami.
Heading straight towards me.
Just leave me be.
But too late I count to three.
Before I become part of the debris.

Daniel Cannop (13)
Bigwood School, Warren Hill

Death Of The Forest

As the trees get sliced down
And the animals hit the ground
Nowhere to go
They just lay around
Death of the forest
Death of the homes
Death of the animals
All that remains
A pile of bones.

High powered noise
The lucky animals flee
No more life in the forest
But one last-standing tree
As its time is at an end
The murderer comes
Comes around a bend.

Crunch and crackle
Trespassers battle
A forest at an end
No more time to spend
Clearing up the mess
Please, no more stress

All life gone forever
An empty forest dull and grey
Now there is just sad, murky water
A cleared scene
All polished and clean.

Natalie Finnie (14)
Bigwood School, Warren Hill

Killing Me Softly

A dark mob of black flies comes over the sky
Isn't it meant to be sunny
Like a real summer?
Crush! The lightning struck
Ferocious droplets tumbled down
Another belt of lightning whipped the flesh on my back,
You are killing me softly
It illuminated a cross perched on a small hill,
She was a mirror image of myself
I remember it clearly
Smash!
She crumbled into tiny fragments
The icy cold liquid wrapped its fingers around me
My soul was drowned into the ground with her
Another part of me had died
My heart crumbled and crushed,
Like a glacier melting
You are killing me softly
Another drop fell,
Fizzed on my skin
I was steaming with uncontained fury,
Releasing all the anger in me
Half my body was buried
Below the cross perched on the hill
You are killing me softly
I remember when I enjoyed the cool drops of water
It felt great on my skin
Why did it have to change?
Don't you know I am fragile?
You use me to shelter you
You never consider my well-being
You are killing me softly
Don't you know I don't rise from the dead?
All you want is to fulfil your selfish needs
Why are you killing me softly?

Natasha Ngonyamo (14)
Bigwood School, Warren Hill

Broken Soldiers

When the night is calm
And our world is at peace,
Shimmering stars float in breathless air
The luminous moon obscured only by stray clouds
Only when we are safe
Must we hear our silent thoughts of danger
Thoughts of betrayal, loss and war.

A war that is two wars since our,
'War to end all wars.'
Our imagination fed stories,
Of hatred, anger and sorrow.
Where death stalks our brave soldiers
As they curse through hot, desert night winds,
Facing, biting, stinging clouds of dust,
Their gun's a loyal companion to them,
Our soldiers get broken, our soldiers get killed,
And for what?

A war that isn't a war,
A war that is to bring peace,
But brings death and destruction.
It's not just our soldiers who suffer.
Their cities shake and thunder with bombs.
Ruined treasures, fogs of smoke.
The crash of glass, children's screams
Where is the hope?
Where is the liberation?

When dawn comes
And the world wakes from its sleep,
We remember what we thought of last night,
We hear of yet another broken soldier.

Sonya Belle (14)
Bigwood School, Warren Hill

Life Needs To Change!

Guns, knives, gun to your head.
There are little kids getting shot dead.
This is a world not made for war
So what are we doing this for?
Stop, think, just look back,
There's little kids following your track.
I think we need world peace.
How would you feel if your kids were like this?
Stop, think, just look around,
Just listen to that crying sound.
She has lost her mum, sister and her dad.
That's why she is always acting bad.
Guns, knives, gun to your head,
Why don't we stop this before we all drop dead?

Dominique Rose (13)
Bigwood School, Warren Hill

Why Me?

I cry all alone
I cry out for help,
But all I hear is the odd dog yelp,
I think and think about what's going to happen next . . .

I always take the blame,
I feel so ashamed,
But what have I done,
I've never understood,
I am so lonely.

There's nowhere to turn.
When I'm feeling down,
They all just stare and give me a frown,
So please help me,
Wherever you are,
I've made it this far, and I just can't take it anymore.

Louise Banister (14)
Bigwood School, Warren Hill

Abuse Over The World

My name is Kate, I'm only five,
To tell the truth I wish I wasn't alive.
Every day I live a lie, having to deny,
The overwhelming pain is too much, but I have to keep it inside.
The teacher asks questions, have to make excuses
'Young Kate dear where did you get those bruises?'
Home that night Daddy's still at work
Try to creep upstairs, Mummy goes berserk.
She pulls me back down with my hair,
Calls me names, does she ever care?
Punch after punch I sit and cry,
Hear keys turn in the door, I run upstairs to hide
Daddy comes upstairs, I ask him why
Why Daddy, why do you want me to die?
It all went dark, he beats me for the cheek
I start to imagine others like me.
On the other side of the world a boy just like me,
Is suffering the consequences of slavery
I read about him in a book at school,
When we were learning about how the world was so cruel.
Not getting paid for his work, they treat him like dirt
Whipped and abused if he doesn't agree
In some senses he reminds me of me.
I opened my eyes, it hurts to breathe
I'm in the hospital on a respiration machine
My parents lied, said I fell down the stairs
All I know is when I get home the abuse will start again.

Rebecca Allen (14)
Bigwood School, Warren Hill

One Cut Too Many

Pile up mascara
Darken the eye
Last look in the mirror
And into the night.

Out in the cold
No one to call
Alone in the world
Her tears start to fall

Pull out a tissue
A dab here and there
A thought comes into mind
Does anyone care?

A blade in her hand
Adrenalin pumps
She makes one neat cut
And feels her heart thump

She carries on cutting
Crying in pain
Removing her anger
But what will she gain?

Her body in shreds
Crying out for help
She makes one final gash
And lets out a yelp

She falls to the ground
Her body stained red
It was one cut too many
Now she is dead.

Natasha Thompson (14)
Bigwood School, Warren Hill

Can The Past Be Changed?

The winter breeze bit my skin.
The wind's icy fingers clinched onto my entire body.
An overcast hung in the sky.
The minute moon replaced the sun
The sand on the bank evaporated
The sea rushed up to the shore
Can the past be changed?
The intense noise haunted me.
I stood . . .
Still as a statue, hard as bricks, tough as nails.
The controversial, ever changing world stood before me.
Fear tickled my senses
Can the past be changed?
Rocks crunched, snapped and crumbled.
Waves hit me cautiously.
Bubbles slithered slowly up my leg.
Tensing my heart.
My soul drowned.
My mind clogged.
My heart raced round the track of blood.
Speeding past all major organs
The drums pounding in my heart catch up with me
I choke to unblock my throat
Gas takes over
My patchy brain begins to fade.
Gathering a cluster of guts
I begin walking
Walking into the misty air.
There is no sunrise.
No sunset
No beginning
And no end
Can the past be changed?
The sea rises
Reaching high
No separation between it and the sky.
I don't know where to go
Which way do I turn?
All I know is that I am last
One of a kind.

One in a million.
Aware of the fatal fall ahead
Time for me to end this.
It looks like the time has come
Not like when the world begun.
Can the past be changed?
The gas begins to strangle me
There is no door, I have no key
Death!
Death is corrupting my throat
Feels as if death is begging my fate.
There's no escape
I must admit
I search the heavens
They remain unlit
After watching the charging sea
Building up
I realise
I take the step
There's no one to turn to
Just one simple step forward
Any last words? I ask myself
My mind trembles.
All I can think is
Did anyone care?
Does anyone care?
All the warnings
All the stress
I should've known better
Cleared up the mess
Pollution
Global warming
Global dimming
Oil extraction
Metal extraction
Climate change
Burning fuels
Acid rain
Burning hydro carbons
Quarrying
Litter
It's bitter

Something could've been done
Should've been done
Fear, fear, fear
It's always there.
Can *you* change the past?
Now it's too late
Or is it?

Chantice Kyle (14)
Bigwood School, Warren Hill

Pollution

Why, oh why, does man pollute?
To the man who did this I will not salute.
Pollution's wrong
Very wrong
It's just like a man wearing a thong
CO_2 kills the o-zone
Turn off the fire in your home.

Pollution's not a crime
Although you should do your time,
But your time will pass,
But not the o-zone
For that's not refundable
You can't take CO_2 back
It's stuck there forever
It's stuck there forever
Man has finally made his mark
Turn to thirty with a click
If you start to recycle
It will help the atmosphere
Dump the car, pick up the bike
For this world only has a certain amount of *time!*

Ben Sharpe (12)
Bigwood School, Warren Hill

RIP

If you saw someone dying in the street,
Would you give them what they need?
Would you let them suffer if you knew it was someone's brother?
Would you think of the family who were living happily?
Would you think of their pain or would you think it was a game?

Would you be there carrying his coffin or would you carry on scoffing?
How many people will it take?
How many families will you break?

Remember one thing, sons are for life.
Let's hope to God, yours don't fall under the knife.

Robyn Squires (12)
Bigwood School, Warren Hill

People

People, people please
Change CO_2 because
CO_2 is killing more
Than World War II.

Why ride a motorbike
If it's giving off fumes?
And why ride a car or a bike
If it's killing me as well as you?

Why do it?
Please think about nature and others
You're killing hundreds of thousands
Even millions in seconds
Because of those fumes.

Adam Rycroft (12)
Bigwood School, Warren Hill

Animal Cruelty

I'm all in the dark
No one around me
I'm so scared
Four walls surround me

My friends have all gone
I'm the only one left
The people took them
But I don't want to be a pest

There's only four bars
That lead me to light
I wish I was out there
Looking at the stars at night

I hope it's not too late
Before I go too
Maybe there's a way out
Of this horrendous zoo

Well this is goodbye
Maybe for a lifetime
You can't hear my voice
Even at night-time.

Cloe Lane (11)
Bigwood School, Warren Hill

Abuse

Why do people do it? It's not nice at all.
Children come home from school and get battered to the floor
When you wake up in the morning your arms are all sore.

Latisha Ffrench (11)
Bigwood School, Warren Hill

Girlfriend Punchbag

He used her as a punchbag
He used her as a toy
He used her for pleasure
What a horrible boy

The neighbours saw bruises
They dare not ever ask
'Bout the cuts and scratches
It was his daily task

Soon it got worse
Throwing around
They asked what was wrong
'I fell on the ground'

Scared to leave him
Scared to talk
Thrown by the hair
Now she can't walk

With each leg broken
With each arm cracked
Poor Lizzie Walker will never be back.

Rebecca Thorpe (11)
Bigwood School, Warren Hill

Ouch!

Ouch,
Mummy please stop it
I can't take it any longer,
The pain is getting stronger,
What have I done?
Is it really fun
To hurt your own child?

You've thrown lots of chairs,
And me down the stairs.
I can't take it any longer,
The pain is getting stronger,
What have I done?
Is it really fun,
To hit your own child?

Abi Simpson (12)
Bigwood School, Warren Hill

Recycling

R ecycle, to save the
E arth and the decreasing population of most of the
C reatures on the planet.
Y es, please recycle, it does help the
C reatures to
L ive easier lives and hopefully lower the
I ncreasing heat of the planet.
N ever forget, the planet can't stand the amount of pressure we
G ive to it.

Penny Adams (11)
Ellesmere Port Specialist School Of Performing Arts, Ellesmere Port

Litter Is Terrible

L eave our planet tidy
I t is disrespectful
T ry to recycle
T he planet needs our help
E arth is not our rubbish dump
R ecycle don't litter.

Kelly Tranter (12)
Ellesmere Port Specialist School Of Performing Arts, Ellesmere Port

Litter

You see it on the ground,
It is all around.
It is called litter,
It is so bitter.
Don't drop it here
Don't drop it there.
Put it in the bin
You're polluting the world.
Be kind to everyone
Put it in the bin.

Bethany Francis (12)
Ellesmere Port Specialist School Of Performing Arts, Ellesmere Port

Litter

I begin to see litter everywhere
I know it's sudden but it has to end!
Instead of putting it around the bend
Put it where it belongs, in the recycling bin.

Sophie Gore (12)
Ellesmere Port Specialist School Of Performing Arts, Ellesmere Port

Homeless

It's a hard thing being homeless,
It's like they all couldn't care less,
With bloody hands and a muddy dress,
It's a hard thing being homeless.

Nobody cares or looks after me,
I have to shelter under the oak tree,
When I have scratches on my face and blood on my knee,
Nobody wants or looks after me.

The school kids all shout things and I know it's all true,
In my world the sky's black,
In theirs it is blue
I try to ignore it but I know it's all true.

Being homeless I get depressed,
This can cause drugs, self harm and stress,
I try to avoid it but my life's a mess,
My life's not worth living.
Being *homeless!*

Claire Purcell (12)
Ellesmere Port Specialist School Of Performing Arts, Ellesmere Port

Recycle

Litter, litter on the ground,
Pick it up and move around,
Find a bin,
And put it in,
Everyone recycle with me,
And you will get a gift for free,
To recycle is the best,
It saves the world from lots of mess.

Deanna Prout (11)
Ellesmere Port Specialist School Of Performing Arts, Ellesmere Port

Homelessness

Most of us are very lucky
Have a roof over our heads
But some of us live on the streets
As one of my best friends said
Sleeping in the gutter
Sleeping in the rain
The most horrible thing
We can think of is being in terrible pain
So come on and put homeless people back in a home
And next time it's raining or snowing,
Please don't moan!

Stephanie Bean (12)
Ellesmere Port Specialist School Of Performing Arts, Ellesmere Port

Save The Day

Global warming,
Warm and hot,
Recycle the world,
In a plastic pot,
Global warming,
Hot in the sky,
Global warming, why?
Litter on the ground,
Which does pollute,
Killing creatures,
Which are cute,
Global warming,
Has gone a long way,
Why not help us,
Save the day.

Chris Wilson (12)
Ellesmere Port Specialist School Of Performing Arts, Ellesmere Port

Story Of A Plastic Bottle

Paper, bottles, tins and glass jars and cardboard thrown
On the rubbish tip
Dumped on the side of the road.
Ever thought what happens to your rubbish?
Chucked in the dustbin left for a week
Flies all over me
Then to the bin lorry
Now with rotting waste
Dumped in a landfill
Stuck here for years
Plastic bottles take a long time to biodegrade
If only I was recycled.
I could be something new
By now.

Jessica Williams (12)
Ellesmere Port Specialist School Of Performing Arts, Ellesmere Port

Homeless Life

Life is hard when you are homeless
A terrible place to be,
Especially when you're on your own without your family.
Life is hard when you're homeless,
Life gets harder by the day
And you're trying to find what to do,
Wishing it all goes away.

Jamie Boyle (12)
Ellesmere Port Specialist School Of Performing Arts, Ellesmere Port

How Would You Feel?

Just imagine if you were on the street
No money, no comfort, no heat
Imagine sleeping in a cardboard box
With nothing to eat and a tatty old sheet
Imagine being labelled as a tramp
With not even a tent so you can camp
How would you feel?

Natasha Flinn (12)
Ellesmere Port Specialist School Of Performing Arts, Ellesmere Port

Rubbish Rage

Rubbish, rubbish on the floor
There is now a blockage by the door
Put it, put it in the bin
You will help our world live for longer.
This will make us feel much stronger
Save our environment, let us live and forgive.
We need our world!

Emma Jones (12)
Frodsham College, Frodsham

The Green Side Of Life

Litter is everywhere
But people don't seem to care
They don't know what they are doing
But they know there's a dirty smell in the air
Litter causes a lot of damage.
So don't be cruel or mean.
Or you just don't know, you might be seen.
So please don't be on the dark side,
Be on the green side of life.

Elliott Prendergast (13)
Frodsham College, Frodsham

Recycle

Don't be mean
Just go green
Don't be gay
Recycle today
Don't be lame or be ashamed
Take notice of the world one day
Plastic bottles
Paper bags
Empty packets of ciggies and fags,
The planet is wasting
It's wasting away, so come on and change it today.
You can change it, you know you can
So recycle that empty can
We can make the planet better if you care
So come along if you dare!

Emily Davies (12)
Frodsham College, Frodsham

That One Bad Bet

The man stood on the street dripping wet
He had lost all his money on a twisted bet
All he had left was a thin, torn jacket
And an empty scrunched up chocolate bar packet
He watched the people walk on past
Going to their places extremely fast
Cold, wet and alone he stumbled over a stuck up stone
Now lying on the floor
His dead body moves no more
Later the next day his body had gone away
There one day, gone the next
He got himself into that awful mess.

Eloise Edwards (13)
Frodsham College, Frodsham

Global Warning!

Environment, environment! Just stay green.
Pick up the rubbish and keep it clean.
Paper, bottles, rubbish, fags.
Pick them up and put them in bags.
Ice is melting, the world might end,
Come on guys.
You should attend.
This is the world you live in,
So make it a better place.
Recycle, bin rubbish.
Let's not keep it a messed up trace.
Cars, vans, polluted air.
People just really need to care.
Animals dying, global warming.
Come on everyone!
It's a massive . . .
Warning!

Lucy Wallbank (13)
Frodsham College, Frodsham

Rainforests

The rainforests are becoming ruined,
Trees are falling,
Bugs are crawling, but not for long.
If we carry on this way,
The rainforests will go.
All the animals in them,
Will soon go away.
Is this right?
We should try and stop this,
You can stop littering
And turn off lights.
Save the rainforests.

Neena Tamber (12)
Frodsham College, Frodsham

A Dark Green Poem

A very Earthly scream
Agony and fury
She couldn't take anymore
This was the end of the story.

She hit mankind
With all her might
Storms and curses
Icy, piercing light.

With the sympathy of stars
She punished and plundered
Destroying her destroyers
Whilst onyx clouds thundered.

We were the ones who began the debt
So we were the ones to pay
With our evolution becoming deadly
The Earth suffered in every way.

So you children of the planet
This is now the bitter end
Perhaps you'll be lucky and get another chance
And you'll learn to be the planet's friend.

Forest Onderka-Lang (14)
Guilsborough School, Guilsborough

Global Warming

It makes us mad
Because it's bad.
It hurts us inside
Because it makes us cry.
It gets worse everyday
So it makes us pray,
For a better day.
It needs to stop
Because it's bad for us lot.

Sophie Humphries (13)
Guilsborough School, Guilsborough

CO$_2$ Act!

Here we are, in 2008
Most of the things are great
But sadly there is one thing
The global warming!

At the end of the day everyone knows
One day the Earth will blow
With pollution everywhere
It sure gives me a scare!

The polar bears have to swim everyday
I can tell you this, it's no play
Ice caps melting all the time
This is all our crime!

One day the animals may go
This will happen in all one blow
If we make an act to save our home
At the end it won't be a moan.

At the end it will save our life
No complaints, no strife
Cut down on CO$_2$, recycle, help
In the end it will help so
Our world will be safe and emissions low!

Leena Sharma (13)
Hall Green Secondary School, Hall Green

O' Wildlife

Trees, trees, trees o' trees
Don't knock them down it's the house for bees
Bushes are always green
It's where beans grow, eat them and it will make you very, very mean.

Underground is the house to weasel
They only run when they drink diesel
It's all about wildlife
So don't mess around on the street playing with a knife.

There are many animals
So humans watch out for cannibals
Watch out for the heat
Watch out for pollution and animals,
Then you will still be able to eat meat.

If you can't bear the hotness
It will wipe you out and leave the world spotless
Leaves grow on wood
Make sure you don't mess up your life dealing and smoking bud.

So remember them summertimes
Having watery mouths when you look at that tree full of juicy limes
Waking up to seeing the sun shine its rays
Counting how much longer is left, counting day by days.

So people hate it when it rains
Overflowing and blocking drains
Getting angry when it's cold
People are like *ha ha* you're going to feel it more
Because you're bold.

Suhayl Iqbal (13)
Hall Green Secondary School, Hall Green

Extinction

There once was a creature called a Caspian tiger,
Until the last one died in a cage.
It did nothing wrong - only to survive.
But this only enflamed the farmer's rage.

Now the elephants are heading that way,
Eating crops just to get by.
But the farmers don't want them unless they're dead.
Are we really going to let all these poor creatures die?

Us humans are mostly the cause,
So maybe we're the solution.
Most of this can be blamed on us,
It's our fault for this extinction.

Amy Musgrave (14)
Kirkby College, Kirkby-in-Ashfield

What Are We Doing?

We always seem to be,
Destroying the world as far as we can see.
Pollution causes the climate to change.
In so many ways that it has its own range.
Millions of people constantly dropping litter.
I think it makes the world bitter.
Recycling will help to save the rainforests and stop animal extinction.
All of this comes as a prediction,
In which it shows a dark world coming to an end
All of this is just around the bend.

Megan Abrahall (14)
Kirkby College, Kirkby-in-Ashfield

Help

Our planet is being totally destroyed,
It has gone so far it will be hard to avoid,
And if it takes that route the fault is all our own,
Because of the care and respect that was never shown,
To the beautiful life from death through till birth,
And the planet we live on, the planet called Earth.

For this place is more special than we'll ever know,
The only place in the solar system where things breathe and grow,
From fish to birds and eight legs to none,
If we don't stop now these creatures are gone.

So turn off a plug and switch off a light,
To help make our future try and look bright,
And respect the animals, don't let them die out,
For if we do nothing there will be no doubt
That an end will come to the sea and the land,
As the structure of life holds on by a strand.

Ailish Dalton-Winfield (14)
Kirkby College, Kirkby-in-Ashfield

Green Peace

The globe is getting sweaty,
Just like my Auntie Betty
Ice caps are melting,
Animals are dying
Trees are falling but
Cars are still driving
The oceans are polluted,
The rainforests are deteriorating
But what are we doing to save our world?

Adam Gage (13)
Kirkby College, Kirkby-in-Ashfield

Destroy All Beauty

War and debate,
Changing my heart rate,
Ruin our world,
And suffer the consequences.

Change our world,
For the better,
A girl may try,
So please just let her.

It doesn't take much,
It could be part of your day,
To make pollution,
Go away.

Change your lifestyle, it could be better.
For the world might not let go.

Dean Kennedy (14)
Kirkby College, Kirkby-in-Ashfield

Do Your Bit

The Earth is being destroyed fast,
So do your bit to make it last,
Just turn off the light.
Unplug the TV,
Walk to the place you wish to be,
Please do your bit to make it last,
Hurry up and do it fast!

Melissa Tyler (14)
Kirkby College, Kirkby-in-Ashfield

One World

There's only one world.
But yet we *choose* to ruin it.
Global warming, pollution and poverty.
These are all caused by us.
There's only one world.
But yet we *choose* to ruin it.
Racism, war and genocide.
We do and have always discriminated others but why?
There's only one world.
But yet we *choose* to ruin it.
Once it's gone, it's gone.
End of.

Alice Warren (14)
Kirkby College, Kirkby-in-Ashfield

War And Peace

W e wish for peace
A nd we don't get it.
R ound the world.

A fghanistan,
N ear Iraq.
D own with war.

P eace to the world.
E arth needs less violence
A nd death.
C ome and protest for the
E arth's sake.

Jessica Playford (12)
Kirkby College, Kirkby-in-Ashfield

Litter And Recycling

L itter everywhere
I t's destroying
T he world,
T here is global warming
E verywhere
R ecycle and reuse.

A polar bear with no home
N ext there will be more
D ue to global warming.

R escue the world
E xtinction will be near
C aused by you
Y oung
C hildren
L ittering
I t's
N ot
G ood for global warming.

Patricia Hartley (13)
Kirkby College, Kirkby-in-Ashfield

Save Our World

Don't fill the world with litter
Make it gleam and glitter
Help the planet, can't you see?
Save the green forest canopy
Make the world green and free
Help save our community
Being homeless isn't great
So lose the plastic bags and don't tempt fate
Can't you see our planet's warming
Come on people get the warning!

Bethany Atkin (12)
Kirkby College, Kirkby-in-Ashfield

What Is The World Coming To?

What is the world coming to?
I really haven't the slightest clue

A lot of war, racism and fighting,
I couldn't really put it down in writing.

Rainforests are being chopped down,
Enough to make any animal frown.

The world's hotting up because of climate change,
Temperatures in their highest range.

Extinct animals never coming back,
It's down to humans we deserve a smack.

Poverty and homeless around the world,
When I heard this my stomach curled.

Recycling all of the world's litter,
If it's left lying around, it seems really bitter.

The world's being destroyed due to pollution,
Surely to all of this there is a solution.

Tia Elvidge (13)
Kirkby College, Kirkby-in-Ashfield

Recycling

R ecycle and reuse,
E xtinction will be soon,
C hildren can help too
Y ou can,
C ause litter,
L et's take care of the Earth,
I n everything we do,
N ot to cause harm
G ive it a go, *recycle!*

Bethany Osborne (12)
Kirkby College, Kirkby-in-Ashfield

The Big Wide World!

Our world is a mess
It wasn't made like that
We need to pull together
Pull a new world out of the hat
How do we do this?
May you ask
It's easy really
Just a simple task.
These little things
Can make a difference
We can stop the pollution
Right this instance
Please make things better
In every possible way
Everything you do
Makes the world better every day.

Demi-Jay Lound (12)
Kirkby College, Kirkby-in-Ashfield

The Forgotten Voices Of WW2

F ear
O utrage
R emembrance
G enocide
O bliteration
T error
T ermination
E xecution
N azi

V ictims
O ffence
I njustice
C oncentration camp
E nemy
S wastika.

Lucy Stendall (14)
Kirkby College, Kirkby-in-Ashfield

Look Over There

Look over there
Someone would say,
Let's go hit him,
And tease him all day.

He's different, not like you or me,
He's black,
He's white,
He's red you see.

Look over there,
He's got funny hair,
It's big and puffy,
Let's give him a stare.

He's different, not like you or me,
He's black,
He's white,
He's red you see.

Look over there,
That boy's running home,
I didn't realise at school,
How he's always alone.

He's different, not like you or me,
He's black,
He's white,
He's red you see,
But still he's the same as you and me!

Shannon Owens (12)
Kirkby College, Kirkby-in-Ashfield

Cheeky Beggars

There are lots of beggars on our streets
Throw some money at their feet.
The Big Issue they try to sell
Just go away! We all yell
Next day they try again
Just to get a bit of change.

Billy Beaver (12)
Kirkby College, Kirkby-in-Ashfield

Mother Earth!

Global warming isn't hard to explain,
It leaves Mother Earth crying with excruciating pain.
Watching the world go by,
When the changes leave us all in sorrow and dismay,
We need to stop it now so the temperature doesn't rise.
This hurts our planet in every single way,
As our Planet Earth is precious and can't be replaced,
We need to act now or our home will be erased.

Sophie Pitchford (12)
Neston High School, Neston

Never Forget Them

P eople dying,
O bviously it's not right.
V ery little they own,
E vidence is all around.
R eact and help them.
T alk to others and spread the word.
Y et life goes on.

Rebecca Washington (14)
Neston High School, Neston

Climate Change Say No!

Eating away at the polar
Ever thought of going solar
Or even it could be wind
Fossil fuels have to be binned.
Water levels are flowing high
Why don't you reach into the sky.

Did you know carbon kills?
We don't want any oil spills
Imagine you're in the polar
Stuck in the moment without wind or solar
Want to hear about nuclear?
Do you know? Are you sure?
How would you like to be in a disaster?
It's a bit like having ketchup on your pasta
How would you like to be in a flood?
It's like being hit by a sea cat. Imagine the blood
How would you like to be in a drought?
No you wouldn't, let me hear you shout.

Peter Ankcorn (11)
Neston High School, Neston

War

W hat is it good for?
A bsolutely nothing
R ifles, bullets and missiles, we shouldn't do it.

W eapons
A re
R ancid

W hy do we do it?
A ttack each other,
R espect not given.

Connor Jellicoe (12)
Neston High School, Neston

Poor Polar Bears

P erfect snow surrounding.
O ver the snowy ice caps.
L arge white paws printed in the snow
A gitated as the ice blocks melt
R oaring and playing with other polar bears,

B are and empty
E ating raw fish.
A rctic is disappearing
R olling in the last pieces of snow
S now has now gone!

Charlie Rattenshaw (13)
Neston High School, Neston

Animals

A nother species dying.
N ot many people are helping them.
I magine our world without them.
M any species of animals around the globe.
A nimals make the world a fascinating place,
L ocations as habitats around the world,
S ad to see their habitats destroyed.

Dean Norman (12)
Neston High School, Neston

Ice Caps

Polar bears are stuck in ice caps
I want to stop this
Lonely, scared, anxious, future!

Jake Carr (13)
Neston High School, Neston

Trapped

Large scale fishing, trapped under the sea
Trapped under a net
Trapped away from the surface
Trapped away from their friends

Large scale fishing, large scale men
Extinction is close, it's just round the bend
Think about the fish then think of yourself
Think about it, is it worth it, think about the wealth

It's tasty and tender but at a heavy price
6,000 pounds out the sea, for a chop and a slice
You do not fear, you do not panic, you do not cry,
But instead what you do, you begin to fry.

Ben Everitt (13)
Neston High School, Neston

Help The Animals

Animal cruelty in this world
Should be made to cease
So we should join together
To make animal peace.

Animals dream to live happily and safe,
So no one should ever give up faith.

All animals, big and small,
We can save them all.

Donate money, stop the pain,
They all need our help,
This isn't a game!

Katie Nall (14)
Neston High School, Neston

Pollution

P eople change this world every day,
O n most things we do, the environment burns away.
L ike keeping light bulbs on,
L ike leaving the telly on standby,
U nnecessary use of cars, computers and cooking fuels.
T oday, not tomorrow, we need to change,
I mprovements must be made.
O ur world is disappearing,
N ever will be seen again.

Catherine Gould (13)
Neston High School, Neston

Death

D estiny is coming
E xtinction is arriving
A single chance is here now
T rue it may be mean but
H ope is all we have got.

Casper Evans (12)
Neston High School, Neston

Save Us

S tuck on a melting ice cap,
A nd no food or water,
V iewing all that's left of my home,
E vil sun what have you done?

U nmistakably this is our end,
S ave us now before our world ends.

Matthew Lewis (13)
Neston High School, Neston

Untitled

Poor polar bear never makes his bed,
He sleeps on the ice instead,
No blanket, no sheet, no bed to sleep on,
His heavy coat keeps him warm,
Warm, warm, warm.

They are worried about the ice melting
Nowhere to go and live
No food for his family
He's got nothing to give.

Kelly Cubbins (13)
Neston High School, Neston

Change

Everything is changing,
And we can't last,
Life is not worth living if we can't change fast,
Extinction is near,
And our hearts beat at speed,
Not even God is caring,
Because of our selfish greed.

Dominic Benson (13)
Neston High School, Neston

Racism

R acism is mean
A nd
C ruel
I t doesn't matter what
S kin colour, black or white
M aybe we make it the problem, think!

Chloe Leadbetter (13)
Neston High School, Neston

One Community

Racism turns people against each other,
Don't be abusive, act like a brother
Black and white should come together,
We must be friends forever.
Yes, it does happen in the big game.
The players find it such a pain,
Think before you say
Do the right thing and act today,
Take the opportunity
And come together as one community.

Harry Smith (12)
Neston High School, Neston

Untitled

It's awful
It's disgraceful
It's not cool
It's cruel
It's rank
It's dirty
This is war!

Ben Brothwell (12)
Neston High School, Neston

Changing

Ice is melting
The world getting hotter
Polar bears have got nowhere to go
Climate changing
Mother Nature's rearranging
Everyone needs to help
To make the world a better place
Before the world turns to waste.

Mollie Simmons (13)
Neston High School, Neston

Can You Remember It?

Can you remember it?
The days when you could feel the lush green grass
beneath your paws
The days when you could feel the cold winter winds against
your face as you soared the skies
The days when you could feel the waves pushing and pulling you
backwards and forwards in the tropical seas
The days you could feel the -60 degrees temperature
while climbing the tallest ice cap
The days in the wild.

Can you remember it?
The days where you could look out over the golden African plains
The days where all you could see was dense forest for miles
The days where you could see your young playing
in the tropical reefs
The days where you could see your next meal grazing
just in front of you
The days in the wild.

Can you remember it?
The days where you could smell the forest's beautiful smell
The days where you could smell your prey
The days where you could smell something's territory
The days where you could smell ripe fruit
The days in the wild.

Can you remember it?
The days where you can taste the juiciest berries ever
The days where you can taste fresh insects from inside their nest
The days where you can taste the oily fish that's squirming
in your mouth
The days where you can taste the juicy meat of a fresh kill
The days in the wild.

Can you remember it?
The days where you can hear the rustling of trees
as small monkeys jump through them
The days where you can hear the splash of penguins
sliding into the icy water
The days where you can hear calls of help from dying animals
The days where you can hear mothers calling to their young
The days in the wild.

Can you imagine it?
The days where you can't feel the pain of a bullet in your side
The days where you can't look out and see animals with giant monsters
coming to make a coat out of you
The days where you can't smell the smoke of a gun just been shot
The days where you can't taste the metal bullets in your food
The days where you can't hear the bangs and squeals of guns
being shot at innocent creatures
Already 99.9% of all animals that once lived on this world are now
extinct and we need you to help us not to make it any more!
Because these are the days we're hoping for in the future.

Sophie Roscoe (12)
Neston High School, Neston

Global Warming

G lobal warming is working hard now
L ots of pollution all around us, up high, down low
O pposing the world, the ice caps and you
B attling out oxygen, until it's all gone
A busing the polar bears, the ice caps and you
L eaving a trail for us to foolishly follow

W aiting for a chance to act
A busing the world and all its possessions
R unning free from factories
M aking the world go evil on us
I llustrating with grey, erasing blue,
N ipping away at the ozone layer
G alloping around and around, waiting to kill us one by one.

Ben Stott (12)
Neston High School, Neston

Extinction

Thousands of animals suffering in silence
Many people committing the violence
The roar of the lion, the scream of an ape
The final kill, the last escape.

The homes of creatures torn to shreds
From the nest of a bird to a lion's bed
The strongest of animals reduced to tears.

The cruelty of humans has to end
Animal extinction is just around the bend.

Ryan Traill (14)
Neston High School, Neston

Animal Extinction

Poaching for sport,
Animals getting hurt,
Animals with scars,
The hunters behind bars,
The blood and the pain,
The thunder and the rain.
The shooting and eating,
The animals are pleading,
The gruesome brutality,
The animals' fatality,
Save the animals, save the animals,
And stop the cannibals.

Elliot Banton (13)
Neston High School, Neston

Racism

Separate pieces in a puzzle,
Same pieces just a different colour,
Even in football the one main sport,
Put one foot wrong and you're to blame,
An easy target for bullies to see,
Intimidated, scared it could have been me,
It's just like O and X in the game,
Black and white should be treated the same.

Alice Evans (13)
Neston High School, Neston

Drip-Drop

Drip-drop the rain never stops,
Drip-drop there goes their crops.
Drip-drop the people are weeping,
Drip-drop the children aren't sleeping.
Drip-drop the families are crying.
Drip-drop everyone is dying.

Chris Jones (12)
Neston High School, Neston

War

War changes people's lives
Disagreement is dealt with by knives
Soldiers are sent on the government's say
They might never return one day
Guns rip families to shreds
Innocent men end up dead
Families of soldiers always pray
One day the world will pay.

Joshua Cooke (12)
Neston High School, Neston

Poverty

P overty is reality
O r can we make it fantasy?
V ery sick people, hardly alive
E veryone and anyone can make a difference
R eal respect is needed for this situation
T oday could change lives
Y ou can help.

Some people are poor because they don't have family or friends,
Richness isn't always about money.

Edward Williams (12)
Neston High School, Neston

Racism And Me

Please stop all racism
It hurts me a lot
My pride in my race
Is all that I've got

Please stop the racism
It hurts my friends too
We all should be friends
And that includes you

Please stop the racism
Because if we do
The world will be happier
And we will be too.

Wesley Osunjimi (12)
Neston High School, Neston

Alone And Lost

Alone and lost,
The baby polar bear fights through the frost,
No one there, nowhere to go,
Walking through the thick white snow.
Wondering what was happening,
Listening to the sound of icebergs snapping.

Ellie Jones (12)
Neston High School, Neston

Deforestation

Dazzling plants dying,
Happy sparkling animals dying
All because you are polluting
The world and the rainforests.
Chopping down the rainforests to grow crops.
Deforestation.

Grace Johnson (13)
Neston High School, Neston

The Big Green Machine

Recycling's easy
Every little helps
If we all pull together
We can improve the world for the better
Pollution is bad
It destroys our air
Let's stop pollution
Or don't you care?

Georgia Macey (13)
Neston High School, Neston

Global Warming

Man has created a hole in the sky
Sending gas and pollution up high
Made worse by the car and travels afar
And the planes that we like to fly
Now nature is taking its turn
The sun continues to burn
The temperature rises, tides flow
Land boundaries are changing we learn
Penguins and polar bears are in need
Their homes are melting indeed
Help is at hand from the new world land
But destroyed by human greed.

Matthew Davies (13)
Neston High School, Neston

Brazil

The country Brazil has a lot of people in poverty.
England takes things for granted, just like you and me.
Parts of Brazil are rich but most of it is poor.
We can put an end to this you and me.
We can put an end to poverty.
I don't understand, why we all day,
Don't think of Brazil in any way.
We can put a stop to this, you and me,
We can stop this catastrophe.

Jonathan Lee (13)
Neston High School, Neston

Flooding

Flooding around your walls,
It's already too late,
Rising from the floor
It creeps through your door.
Water up to your ankles,
A black cat soaked and in distress.
Flowing down the street
Carrying belongings and wheat.
Evicted from your home
And forced into poverty.
Only if global warming could be paused
And all the destruction that I caused.

Jack Daker (13)
Neston High School, Neston

Melting Ice Caps

There was once a place called the Arctic
Most of it's gone now.
So come on George Bush take a bow.
Polar bears are dying
And seals too.
So now think about if it happened to you.
The Earth's getting warmer.
Soon it'll be like a sauna.
That means the water will get higher
As the days go on the ozone layer will tire
Which means the Earth will soon be on fire.

Andrew Adams (13)
Neston High School, Neston

Melting Ice, There Will Be Gaps

Pollution, gas and things like that
The place where polar bears sat.
The ice caps melt as fast as ice cream
When we think about it, we have a bad dream
We want these animals as pets
Then we wonder how many are left.
I am afraid there is still more
Some news that will make you soar,
The water that is kept under the ice
Will roll into our homes as fast as a dice.
So this is what you can do
To make sure cows keep saying moo.
When you are not in a room, turn off the light
Go outside and see colours of delight.
Instead of driving, go for a walk.
You and your friends can have a good talk.
It is upsetting I know
I feel the same way so
The smallest you can do can go a long way.
Do not be afraid to speak out and say.
What might happen today
It could happen any day.

John Collins (13)
Neston High School, Neston

Dying

Luscious green trees dying,
Sparkling fresh water polluted,
Wonderful animals dying,
Happy people dying.
All of this is done by you!
Deforestation.

Emily Egner (13)
Neston High School, Neston

Evanescence

Darkness surrounding me
My blood accelerating
My limbs are bound by shackles of fear
Restoring a little recognition
And for what purpose?
What reason do these pathetic insulters have against me?
Am I just anonymous to them?
Am I really so insignificant?
But what does it matter?
Because I will always have the opportunities they miss
I will stand up for my faith
However hard they pin down my differences
However thick the copper taste of hate lingers in my mouth
I will carry on living the way I want to
For what anticipation is there
When some are too stubborn to listen . . .?

Catherine Williams (13)
Neston High School, Neston

Far Away From Home

Back of dark alleys
Underground,
My whole world is spinning round
Think
Can you imagine?
Staring and scared.
Empty and alone.
My 3 year old brother,
Begging, crying, wants to go home.
Think
I miss my mum
Think.

Sophie Toll (13)
Neston High School, Neston

The Environment

As the Earth's lifespan runs down,
Are we doing enough in our towns?
And when you drop litter on the floor
It will end up on the shore
This will kill animals
Like a box of cannonballs.
Helping the environment is boring.
But it does help pollution rates from soaring.
In the future we want to enjoy our life.
Just like you enjoyed yours!
So save on gas, water and electricity
And make our world one big green city!

Daniel Foulkes (13)
Neston High School, Neston

Climate Poem

C andent
L andscape
I ce caps
M elting
A nd
T omorrow
E very

C ap
H as gone
A stray
N ow
G et
E verybody moving!

Sean Colley (13)
Neston High School, Neston

Recycle

It is the year 2075,
And we are all walking on rubbish,
Plants, animals, they are no more,
The world is one great big dump,
This is all because we didn't recycle.

Lakes are brown,
Hundreds of metres deep,
Just from the melted polar regions,
This is all because we didn't recycle.

Our actions now,
Can shape the future,
Is this how you want it to be?

Alicia Webb (13)
Neston High School, Neston

How Can You Save Our Earth?

How can *we* save our Earth?
You know, we could switch off the lights.
How can *we* save our Earth?
Let's hope the dark doesn't give you a fright.

How can *they* save our Earth?
Animals in forests are dying.
How can *they* save our Earth?
All for the sake of the wood we're buying.

How can *you* save our Earth?
You could have a shower instead of a bath.
How can *you* save our Earth?
Come on, let's make a greener path.

Stop. Think . . . How can you save our Earth?

Jenni Potter (13)
Neston High School, Neston

Go, Go Green Poem

Go, go green, make litter extinct,
The world has changed, don't make it stink,
Animals are dying, let them live,
Don't make them extinct,
Reduce the paper you use and save a tree for an animal to use.
Everything you waste,
Will help poverty win the race,
But everything you use will give a family a place to snooze.
Next racism is bad, it makes the people sad,
It happens at school,
Don't you think it's so cruel?
Turn racism in,
It's got to go in the bin,
Doesn't matter the colour of your skin,
Racism is bad.
Everyone can help to make the world a better place,
Just give the world a chance and you will win the race.

Ashley Davies (13)
Neston High School, Neston

Stop

Where are the animals?
Where is their home?
The animals need to roam
The rhino, the mountain lion
Even the crocodile
The land wasted
Nothing will grow
So it's gone for evermore,
If we don't stop
The loggers, the miners
Even the farmers
Will leave the land to rot
It has to *stop*.

Aimee Thompson (13)
Neston High School, Neston

The Changing World

Rippling water all around,
Freezing winds rushing round and round,
As cold as the snow on the frozen ground,
The polar bear's home is melting!

Swinging, swirling, from branch to branch,
Around the jungle floor he pranced,
Rustling leaves and jungle sounds,
The orang-utan's home is dying!

King of the jungle is his name,
Hunting for food on the Asian plain,
Watching his food with his beady eyes,
He jumps, he leaps, he catches his prize!

Please help to save their world!

Laura McGrath (12)
Neston High School, Neston

End Of War

A man lies on a murky street
Bones sticking out from nothing to eat
His hair is overgrown, malted and coarse
Beaten, bloody and blue from a cruel force.

Another soldier dead, for what?
To prove how much power his country has got.
Let's work together and make war cease
Instead have justice, love and peace.

Tara Hatton (13)
Neston High School, Neston

Melting Ice

M y feet slipping, as my world collapses before my eyes.
E scaping but with nowhere to go
L ying miserably, knowing it's the end of my journey.
T rying to get out of this horrible nightmare
I t's over, no more ice.
N ever to be seen again.
G one and dead.

I ce caps are vanishing, so are the animals.
C an't you see?
E xtinction is closer than we think.

Jaimie Sadler (12)
Neston High School, Neston

What Do We Do?

We all do it every day
To do this we have to pay.
If you could just see what you do
Then maybe you could do what you want to.

The water was once a beautiful place
But destroyed by the human race
If you could go there back in time
Then maybe you could see it in its prime.

You cannot see it with the naked eye
But you may see it in the sky.

Matthew Rigby (12)
Neston High School, Neston

War

Bang, crash, all around,
Cries, weeps, always a sound,
Shelters pouring, no one in sight,
Lights around, all day and night.

Buildings ruined, everything gone,
Nothing seen till the smoke has gone.
People dead, little alive,
Not to know who will survive.

One to one, countries battle,
Destroying the buildings that people settle.
Shot, slaughtered, blood everywhere,
Dying slowly since blood is so rare.

Food short, hungry as ever,
Rations so small, worse than ever.
Painful sounds, disgusting smells,
Firing bombs and exploding shells.

All over, families reunite,
Saving this one and happy night.
Dancing up in that wonderful leather,
Hoping they'll stay together forever.

Eleanor Newall (13)
Neston High School, Neston

Dolphins

Endangered species
Water mammal
Jumps high
Swims fast
Splashes loads
Gentle friends
Smart creatures
Moves swiftly
Leaps miles
Free animals.

April Plant (13)
Neston High School, Neston

Untitled

Endangered species
Bamboo snapper
Tree climber
Unusual markings
Roly poly
Rare breeder
Extra thumb
Lucky symbol
Proud caller
Beautiful animal
Need to save . . .

Sarah Ellis (13)
Neston High School, Neston

Racism

Does it matter what colour I am?
A colour is a colour.
Don't judge me
Because I'm not like you.
Black or white we are all the same,
You call me names that drive me insane.
So much pain, yet you get no gain,
Please stop, it's not fair.
You can't judge me by the colour of my hair.
A colour is a colour, nothing more, nothing less.
Let's stop this stress.

Lauren Hawksford (14)
Ridgeway High School, Prenton

Brain Bender

This poem is about the world in all its splendour,
But the state it's in now is surely a brain bender.
We are portrayed in such wonderful views
With yellows and greens and maybe some blues,
But we can be cruel in several ways
And some people for this can even get paid!
Most of the time we are clean
So we can see where the litterbugs have been.
As you can see I'm no poet,
But look after the world, even you know it!

Stephanie Cragg (11)
Ridgeway High School, Prenton

It's Our Earth

My name is Maria,
I come from South Korea,
So why don't you come over?
But forget your Land Rover.

As big as an elephant,
As heavy as a fat kid,
As round as a ball,
It's only one thing,
It's our home,
It's our Earth.

My name is Charlie,
My favourite singer is Bob Marley,
So why don't you come over,
But forget your mini motor.

As big as a bison,
As heavy as a skyscraper,
As round as a disc,
It's only one thing,
It's our home,
It's our Earth.

Keiran Stanley (14)
Ridgeway High School, Prenton

Street Kid

Alone, cold, nowhere to go,
My self-esteem has gone very low,
I've got no family, no one to turn to,
All I've got, is torn clothes and a shoe,
I owned a stray cat,
Who liked to chat,
His name was Little Pip,
His owners tortured him by a whip,
He liked eating chocolate bars,
But got hit by speeding cars,
I cried for hours,
So I stole him some flowers.

Charlie Evans (12)
Ridgeway High School, Prenton

Our Earth The Bin

Our streets are becoming a bin,
It's so disgusting, it's almost a sin.
It's not just one of us, two or three,
It's everyone, you and me.

The streets are paved with litter,
The stories become so bitter.
They say the end is near,
With litter there and here.

Make our Earth a better place,
Don't throw litter on its face.
People begin to light their candles,
As the Earth is being vandalised and not just by vandals.

The Earth needs help now,
You need to help but how?
The Earth's giving us a loud shout,
Because it's 1, 2, 3 strikes you're out.

Daniel Nall (12)
Ridgeway High School, Prenton

Let's Keep In Pace

The world is a wonderful place
So we have to keep in pace,
Because the climate is changing
So the icecaps are melting.

We have to keep it clean
So we are green.
Don't forget recycling,
We need to start trying.

Stop cutting the trees in the rainforest,
Stop cutting the forest,
Let's save animals from extinction,
Save them from malnutrition.

Racism let's stamp it out,
There is no doubt
They are just like us,
So what's the fuss?

Let's stop the war
What is it for?
It leads to people being homeless,
You could be parentless.

We all have a solution
For the pollution.
But we never do it
So come on let's do our bit.

Why do we have poverty?
It's just a monstrosity.
The world can be a better place
If we all keep in pace.

Amy Griffiths (14)
Ridgeway High School, Prenton

Litterbug!

I'm the litterbug
And I'm here to spread my word,
To help you stop littering
And destroying our pretty world.

So here is a few tips
To help you on your way,
Just quit it now
And that's one thing I have to say.

People drop things everywhere,
So please pick it up,
Put it in the bin
And just be aware.

Pick up that crisp packet,
Don't drop that can,
Consider our future,
It's gonna be bright man.

Look at me in my shades,
Acting all cool
And cling to my chains.

Every day our world needs our help,
So pick up that can
And don't wait for the bin man.

Becky Simpson (12)
Ridgeway High School, Prenton

Pointless Killing

Pointless killing is the name of the game,
Bush and Brown should be put to shame.
The war machines are rolling and ready to go,
The Earth will go in one blow.

The nukes are ready and the soldiers set,
Anyone willing to place a bet
It's all for oil and we joined in
While there in a shelter, where in a bin.

The nukes are off, it's a race to the end,
The nukes are beginning to swerve and bend.

Is this it?
Can it be?
The end of the world, come and see.
Bush and Brown are the ones to blame,
They really should be put to shame.

Dale Longmuir (13)
Ridgeway High School, Prenton

Save The Environment

The grey smoke that made me choke.
The skies full of whirlwinds of smoke.
The litter that makes me sick,
Whilst the sky was really thick.
I walked towards the sea.
The little whales screeching at me.
I couldn't bear it anymore
As I walked along the seashore.
I saw the nets getting dipped in,
Then little whales with broken fins.

Hannah McLaughlin (13)
Ridgeway High School, Prenton

Pollution Our Problem

I drive around in my gas fuelled car
Not realising that I'm no star
I leave my lights on when I'm asleep
When the world is at an end I'll be the one who'll weep
I'll leave the heating on when the door is open
When the ozone is gone I'll be moaning
When I use energy too much today
The Earth will be the one who will pay
I hear, smell, feel and see the change we are in
So put the pollution in the bin.

Dayle Jones (14)
Ridgeway High School, Prenton

Bully Of The Year!

And the award goes to . . .
Don't be a bully
You'd hate it if it was you
Stand up for yourself
And stop the bullying crew

No matter what they say
No matter what they do
Help everyone else
To stop the bullying crew

I know a saying
That will help you through
So listen well to me
And stop the bullying crew

Sticks and stones may break your bones
But names will never hurt you
Remember this throughout your life
And stop the bullying crew.

Alexandria Steele (12)
Ridgeway High School, Prenton

The Big, Big, Green Machine

It's the big, big, green machine
To help the world stay clean
Put your rubbish in the bin
Don't be a sin
Because it's the big, big, green machine
To help the world stay clean
Give to the poor
Don't break the law
Because . . . it's the big, big, green machine
To help the world stay clean.

Katie Rutter (12)
Ridgeway High School, Prenton

Recycle, Recycle!

Recycle, recycle!
You know it makes sense,
Throw it in the bin not over the fence.
Recycle, recycle!
We don't need it anymore,
Throw it in the bin not over the floor.
Recycle, recycle!
When paper's on the floor,
It makes me feel bitter,
They know in their head
They should pick up their litter.
Recycle, recycle!
Please listen to my plea.
Stop the rubbish on this Earth.
Please listen to me.
Recycle, recycle!

Jake Lilliott (13)
Ridgeway High School, Prenton

Change Our World

Street kids are neglected
Royals are respected

People who are murderers
People who are burglars

Poverty and no money
Some things aren't that funny

Everyone deserves a chance
Or at least a second glance

Change our world

All kids with a home
Everybody is well-known

Nobody dies or kills
Nothing stolen, pay the bills

All of us with some money
Always be happy and funny

If I had the chance I would

Change our world.

Hannah Carter-Bloor (12)
Sandbach High School & Sixth Form College, Sandbach

How Our World Can Be A Mean Place

Street children like me
Are never happy
Not loved
Not cared for
Can nobody see?

Out on the streets
It's dusty and dark
With strange noises
And squeaking swings
In the park.

When daytime comes
It's just one of those days
Families together
It makes me gaze.

I wish I was home
In my warm soft bed
Instead of out on the streets
Where it feels like
I'm dead.

Megan Holden (11)
Sandbach High School & Sixth Form College, Sandbach

Street Kids

Tiny fingers, tiny hands
Broken hearts in capital towns

Whatever I do, whatever I say
It won't spin the world another way

There will still be kids upon the street
The parents and kids will never again meet

Tiny fingers, tiny hands
Broken hearts in capital towns

Kids who have to steal to get scraps to eat
Then try and sleep upon a cold street

But together we will have success
We can clear up this awful mess

Whatever we do, whatever we say
We can change their lives, starting today

Tiny fingers, tiny hands
Happy hearts in capital towns.

Isobel Harrop (11)
Sandbach High School & Sixth Form College, Sandbach

What Would Make The World A Better Place?

To make the world a better place
We should all be best mates.
Get rid of drugs, get rid of crime
And find something useful to do with our time.
Bring in fun and happiness,
Get rid of all the dreariness.
People who are upset and down,
Shouldn't fret or frown.
Oh how joyful I would be
If I lived by the sea.
So come along and join with me
And see how happy we can be.

Georgina Innocent-Galletley (11)
Sandbach High School & Sixth Form College, Sandbach

Frightened

Frightened of small spaces I may be
But not as frightened as the dark you see
Frightened of the hand you raise up high
Frightened cos you never understand why
Frightened of the bruises that you leave
Inside and out but no one believes
Frightened of the noises I can hear
Frightened that everyone can sense my fear
Frightened of the future, it's in whose hands?
Frightened of what everyone demands
Frightened of the love I have for you
Frightened of the dreams you did pursue
Frightened of where you'll take me next
Frightened that everything will be vexed
Frightened of the walls that I call home
Frightened when within them, especially alone
Frightened of everything, unforeseen
Frightened of your capability to demean
Frightened of the place I'm safe and sound
Frightened just in case I am found
Frightened of what will be given to me tomorrow
Frightened of the action that will follow
Frightened what will happen if someone reads this
Frightened if your actions still persist
Frightened cos you say it's all my fault
Frightened when you say I can bring it to a halt
Frightened cos you twist things, it's not how it should be
Frightened cos I'm screaming, but no one hears me
Frightened when people look at me in disgust
Frightened when the closest people say I've broken the trust
Frightened of the way you always win
Frightened cos I keep it trapped within
Frightened cos there's nothing I can do
Frightened cos I'm the only one who knows it's *you!*

Jessica Cronshaw (15)
Sandbach High School & Sixth Form College, Sandbach

I Am The . . .

I am the car of the future,
I run on water and never get lost.

I am a house of the future,
I clean myself at no extra cost.

I am a person of the future,
I feel great and I am calm.

I am the wars of the future,
I end myself without any harm.

I am a forest of the future,
I have regrown and I am full of life.

I am the pets of the future
And I defend husband and wife.

I am also the air of the future
And I am fresh and clean.

I am the carbon footprint of the future,
But I hardly exist, I am green.

Who am I?
You may ask.
I am the world of the future
And I live in peace and harmony!

Stephanie Lea (12)
Sandbach High School & Sixth Form College, Sandbach

Why Me?

Why me? I ask
As I walk alone,
It's not my fault
I just had to go.
Rocks are my bed,
All hard and rough,
No family or friends,
It's just not enough.
I need some shelter,
A place to stay,
I don't think it's fair
I live this way.
I cry myself to sleep,
Waking up at every quiet creep.
I'm scared, hungry,
I just don't belong,
I try to get to sleep
By singing a song.
I hear footsteps,
I keep quiet and still,
He kicks and punches
Against my own will.
I run and ask
That question and try to see,
I just don't understand,
Why me?

Rachel Biddle (12)
Sandbach High School & Sixth Form College, Sandbach

What Would Make The World A Better Place?

To stop all wars around the world
To stop the cruelty in every country
Some people that I can trust
That's what would make the world a better place.

No stereotypes to judge you
No bullies to bully you
That's what would make the world a better place.

No rubbish on the floor
No rubbish on the road
The world would be so clean
That's what would make the world a better place.

The world would be a better place if all of this was true
The world would be the best place that I could ever dream of.

Stephanie Bell (12)
Sandbach High School & Sixth Form College, Sandbach

Poor People In The World

Think, just think
Some people have little kinks
In their lives
Husbands and wives
All should be happy
Children wearing their nappies
All eating and drinking
Thinking, thinking
About the food and water they could eat
No shoes on their feet
Rags on their backs
When it rains no macs
So help these people with their lives
Just think again about your lives
And help with their life.

Holly Williams (12)
Sandbach High School & Sixth Form College, Sandbach

Have You Heard Of That Kid?

Have you heard of that kid?
Living on the streets
Begging for food
Begging for money
But he never gets any.

Have you heard of that kid?
Living on the streets
He has no food
He has no home
Just moving from place to place.

Have you heard of that kid?
Living on the streets
He has no food
He has no friends
Just sitting there all alone.

That kid on the streets
Isn't very well
But who cares?
You don't
But I do.

That kid on the streets
Is my friend
I give him money
I give him food
I take care of him.

There are many kids on the streets
Looking for a friend
Someone to care
Someone to take note
So now it's your turn.

Becksy Olpin (12)
Sandbach High School & Sixth Form College, Sandbach

My Poem

Day by day,
night by night,
misty smoke comes into sight.
It puffs out of the factory chimneys
and into the air,
it is far too much for the birds to bear.
If you listen carefully,
you hear hardly any song,
because of the smoke,
the birds have nearly gone.

Day by day,
night by night,
you walk into a room and it is full of light.
TVs on,
it's on loud,
you've left it on,
you must be proud.

CD players blaring,
ever thought of caring
about our little planet?
Water's running,
you're really cunning,
you shouldn't have left it,
let alone ran it.

So there must be a solution
to reduce this pollution.
Our planet is filthy and badly treated,
in a hierarchy table we will be seated,
in the lowest of the low,
that is where we will go,
unless we do something about it,
so please tell everyone and shout it!

This is what we will do . . .
Treat our planet with respect,
don't give animals any neglect,
be good to everything that is living,
be generous, kind and giving.
Reduce the amount of smoke,
help good elderly folk,
use small amounts of water when you go and have a soak.
To me this is no joke.

Really, there is nothing to it,
if I can do it,
so can you!

Charlotte Halliday
Sandbach High School & Sixth Form College, Sandbach

What Would Make The World A Better Place?

Let's help turn the world green,
We all need to be keen,
Let's keep the world clean,
We all need to be seen.

Don't throw rubbish on the floor,
We need to help tidy more,
Let's open a new door
And help those that are poor.

Let's stop bullying once and for all,
Does it really help us? No, not at all,
Don't pick on those who are tall or small,
Let's all come together and have a ball.

Grace Jeffs (12)
Sandbach High School & Sixth Form College, Sandbach

A Better World

The world would be a better place
If we weren't all in each other's face,
We should live our lives and be content
And maybe, maybe we could prevent
Destroying innocent people's lives,
Wives without husbands, husbands without wives,
Kids without parents,
Maybe this can stop
If we take a little time to think about what we've got.

The thing that would make us better people,
The thing,
The thing that makes us want to live,
The thing that makes us move,
The thing that always makes us smile,
Even when we're in a mood,
It makes us want to be the best,
It makes us need to take a rest,
The thing that gives us joy to live,
That's the thing we need.

Kristin Gilmore (12)
Sandbach High School & Sixth Form College, Sandbach

Do Not Be A Litterbug!

Do not be a litterbug!
Open your eyes and look around for a place to put your rubbish.

Not on the street
Or up a tree,
Throw your rubbish in a *bin*.

Bin your rubbish in a *bin*,
Enter your rubbish in a *bin*.

A fun thing to do is to dump your rubbish in a *bin*.

Leave your rubbish in a *bin*,
Invite your rubbish in a *bin*,
Tip your rubbish in a *bin*,
Tap your rubbish in a *bin*,
Even,
Reduce, reuse, recycle if possible

By buying less things with lots of packaging, or by
Using something again,
Go on, don't just sit there, do something . . . *now!*

Lydia Sourbutts (12)
Sandbach High School & Sixth Form College, Sandbach

A Cry For Help

To make this world a better place,
I would only ask one thing,
To get rid of bullies and all people mean,
Forever eternally.

Because no one likes a bully,
Big people strong and bad.

They pick on me, they tease me,
Then they beat me up and stand there,
Stop, admire their handy work,
Glare at me with big beady eyes.

I'm sat there in the corner,
Trying not to look,
While they just laugh and laugh
And then slowly walk away.

But why?
Why?
Why do they do it?
I ask.

I get the point, you're the boss,
You've made it very clear.

Please make the world a better place,
Make them go away.

Because no one likes a bully,
Big people strong and bad.
Please get rid of them.

Lucy Furber (12)
Sandbach High School & Sixth Form College, Sandbach

Illness

Why has this happened?
It's never happened before,
I had a minor heartache,
Then suddenly I fell at the door.

I knew I was ill,
But not this bad,
People treat me differently,
I feel so bad.

They treat me like an alien,
They put me through such pain,
Boom! biggest newsflash,
I'm a lion that's lost its mane.

It's got worse and worse,
I don't feel free,
Maybe it's the end,
The end of me.

I can't believe we've lost her,
We thought there was a cure,
Life's not going to be the same
Without her anymore.

Life without dying,
No more crying,
Life with a smile
That will last for a while,
A better world.

Ellie Doubleday (12)
Sandbach High School & Sixth Form College, Sandbach

How To Make The World A Better Place

Most adults leave it alone
They think it's not their problem
They're making it worse
For the next generation
And the whole nation
Global warming is no joke
It's ruining the planet.

They have nowhere to go
Nowhere to live
Except on the streets
They will be so sad
It's very bad
Street kids need help
It's up to us.

Throwing rubbish on the floor
Making the streets a mess
No one seems to pick it up
It's not good
No one should
Littering is not a good idea
If you see rubbish on the floor
Pick it up.

Bethany Phillips (12)
Sandbach High School & Sixth Form College, Sandbach

Help The World Tick

Help the world tick,
Make it a better place,
Come on let's stick,
We will win the race!

Children on the streets, all alone,
Come on let's give them a caring home,
Let's help the world stick!

Babies crying, hungry, scared,
Loving hearts completely torn,
Come on let's give them love and care,
Let's help the world tick!

Help the world tick,
Make it a better place,
Together we will stick,
We will win the race!

Help us in this world today,
Look after their souls in a caring way,
Let's help the world tick!

So next time you're in your nice warm house,
Think of that child, quiet as a mouse,
Let's help the world tick!

PS you may appreciate what I say,
But nothing will be done until that day!

Hannah Beckett
Sandbach High School & Sixth Form College, Sandbach

Abandoning Is Wrong

Abandoning animals is wrong
Be nice to animals
Animals are getting hungry
No one with you
Dogs trust you are saving them
O nly you can help
No home for pets
It's down to you to save them
No animal will have a bad life if you help save them
Go and *think* about it!

If only there was a way to help them
Save an animal's life now.

What about friendship?
Raining heavily
Outside all alone
Nowhere to go!
Go and do something about it!

Rebecca Hewitt (12)
Sandbach High School & Sixth Form College, Sandbach

Green, Glorious, Green

Green, glorious, green,
We want to save it,
Recycle card or bottles,
Even if it topples.

Climate change - hot or cold,
Litter and pollution,
Save the trees.

Save paper and recycle for The Big Green Poetry Machine,
Animals are becoming extinct and it's not really their fault,
Rainforests are becoming polluted.

Green, glorious, green.

Amita Khera (12)
The Duston School, Northampton

Tropical Trees

All the trees standing tall looking proud and cool,
The monkeys are having fun when they are swinging from vine
                                                        to vine.

Snakes slithering through the spacious ground,
Climbing tree to tree catching prey underground.

When sitting on my chair colouring my person and her hair,
Knowing that people like me are killing animals,
Knowing that everyone is a killer,
People demanding trees for paper,
So there are no animals.

Know that I'm destroying rainforests,
Cutting homes down as quick as a flick.

Birds homes in a factory and no baby bees,
No big green trees,
Now the monkeys are jumping bin to bin,
So now everyone has a sin.

Grace Tredré (12)
The Duston School, Northampton

The Climate Is Changing

The climate is changing all the time,
Even as I'm singing this rhyme.
And you might be in bed
But a monkey could be dead.
So go downstairs and turn everything off
And make yourself a nice warm broth.

The climate is changing all the while,
Even right near the Nile.
The ice is melting, melting
And very soon it will be gone.
So help the world with climate change
Before you reach a very old age.

Terri-Ann Greatorex (11)
The Duston School, Northampton

Save Our World

Look around the world and what do you see?
Pollution, war and poverty.
Do we really realise what it's worth?
Litter, climate change, extinction too.
There are so many things we can do.
We can all do our bit
To stop the world becoming a tip.
Why not recycle, reduce and reuse?
And you'll be the next one on the news.
Think about when you drop that trash
You'll make all the streets look flash
Or maybe consider the people at war,
Remember what they are fighting for.
So really think about our land
And give everybody a helping hand.

Lloyd Butcher (14)
The Duston School, Northampton

Pollution

Pollution is in the air,
It's destroying the ozone layer.
Stop the deodorant cans and the cars.
As the sunlight come down the Earth is getting destroyed.
Everyone is doing this, even the factories and industries.
Let's all think for a second,
Why don't we use less?
Lose pollution and we can all be green.
Soon we may be in danger as there are going to be tidal waves
And tornados a lot more often.
It's getting hotter every day.
Everything is melting like icebergs and ice cubes.
Penguins and polar bears are losing their homes,
So the sea levels are rising, flooding places completely.

Thomas Rust (11)
The Duston School, Northampton

Help Me Or I'll Die

Why are people doing this?
Are they doing it on purpose?
Why do you think this is?
It will harm all of us!

The oil, petrol and digging up holes,
It's making me wary.
Killing the habitats of moles,
It's getting really scary.

It's going all really fast,
I hate it more than you.
No! It's not a blast,
It's terrible times two.

All my resources are being used up,
Like paper, plastic and glass.
Hey you recycle that plastic cup
And quick, do it fast.

It's too late, they ignored us,
I'm going very, very soon.
They didn't want to make a fuss,
But now it's their doom.

Chloe Hunter (12)
The Duston School, Northampton

Animals And Extinction

There is a little polar bear in the Arctic Ocean
And his family is all dead
From this horrible poison.
You only want to kill them for their lovely soft fur
To make a coat for you to buy,
These little cute polar bears have to die.

Melissa Sibley (13)
The Duston School, Northampton

Climate Change

Climate change has just begun,
The animals are going,
Soon there'll be none,
Their numbers are lowering,
Then they're all gone.

The ozone is breaking
While birds are awaking,
Pollution in the making
As the planet is quaking.

Rainforests are being chopped,
And being thrown down the docks,
Little monkeys are dying,
As you turn on the lighting.

So be eco-friendly,
Because you're making our planet die,
We've got to rebuild our planet,
To the way it originally was.

So recycle our planet's resources,
And make it our healthy home once again,
The icebergs are melting,
As the polar bears are belting.

Melissa Barnard (11)
The Duston School, Northampton

War

Needless killing
Families destroyed
Lives ruined
Houses burnt
Buildings bombed
Money wasted
Murders and assassinations

All this for what?

David Whitehead (12)
The Duston School, Northampton

The Poverty Cage

I'm on my own,
I'm all alone,
Goodbye to freedom and love.

I can't escape
The poverty cage,
It's dark and has evil eyes.

But my heart is strong,
It keeps pumping on,
Fighting back the cruelty.

The terror in my eyes is growing stronger
And keeps going for longer and longer,
I feel unsafe . . .
I wish I had a home
To call my own,
Or at least some family to love.

But this is a will
That I will not fulfil
Unless I escape the poverty cage.

Jack Kushniruk (12)
The Duston School, Northampton

A Better Place

Feeling helpless?
Do something about it,
Try recycling, be proud and shout it!

Put your litter in the bin,
Or the animals will get hurt or stuck in.

Pollution is really starting to show,
We're all going to be gone before you know.
Racism is really bad,
It makes some children very sad.

Make our world a better place.

Aleshia Cannell (12)
The Duston School, Northampton

Save The World

Don't destroy our world,
How would we survive?
If people keep on polluting,
Soon no one will be alive.

Poverty and war,
Why are these taking place?
The disagreements and the authority
Are destroying the human race.

Give it a go, don't litter,
Give money to the poor.
You only need to give a pound,
Or two or three or four.

Climate change is drastic
And it's down to our pollution.
But there's hope because recycling
Is just one of many solutions.

So, please join in,
Let's save the world
Then it will still be here,
When you're grey and old.

Joe Burrows (12)
The Duston School, Northampton

Pollution

Litter on the ground,
Animals dying all around.
How will they survive?
Soon there will be none alive.

Dirty air,
Breathed in everywhere.
Oxygen is lacking,
Because of the pollution attacking!

Emily Bustin (13)
The Duston School, Northampton

The Streets

The mess and the rubbish
Makes our country look thuggish,
The ground is all covered,
It really is smothered
In cans and packets
And old soup sachets,
We really are fed up
So help us out and do something about it.

Milk bottle top sand paper bags,
Iron bedsteads, dirty old rags,
Litter on the pavements,
Paper in the streets,
Is this what we really want to see?
No! No! No!

Maddison Jones (13)
The Duston School, Northampton

Global Warming

As Earth is burning
We just decide to keep on turning!

If we decide to let it go
Then the planet will just blow!

Instead of taking the car
Why not walk, it's not that far?

Instead of throwing it in the bin
Recycle the bottles and that tin.

So remember when you read this,
That it is our planet that we dis!

Daniel Dyer (11)
The Duston School, Northampton

Things That Are Changing

Have you noticed these things that are changing
With the pollution, poverty and war?
Everything's getting worse, and we need to change
Because people in Africa are dying for water and begging for more.

We're all getting rich
But some become poor,
Being forced onto the street,
Living on the floor.

Families torn apart by being sent to Iraq,
Fighting for their country, fighting to survive.
Watching the people closest to them die
Whilst families at home hoping they're alive.

All we need to do
Is use a bin
To make a start
In the world we live in.

Laura Leyman (15)
The Duston School, Northampton

Protect Our World

All I can see around the world today
Are wars, poverty and racism.

We can protect ourselves by working together,
No fighting and helping the people who are less fortunate than us.

As well we can help protect our animals,
No killing them just letting them live their own lives.

Next we can recycle, then reuse,
Protect the things that we need to run our world.

Then we can keep our country running as normal,
But we need to get rid of poverty, wars and racism.

Tom Harrison (15)
The Duston School, Northampton

Homeless People

I am homeless, living on the streets,
I wander around the street for something to eat,
I walk around in ripped clothes.

I have no money, I have no friends,
I don't see my family, I don't make a sound,
I can even be underground,
So please take care of me.

Jamie Kelly (11)
The Duston School, Northampton

Global Warming

The sun is getting brighter,
It's producing heat like a lighter.
Trees are being cut down,
All the humans are turning brown,
Homeless people sit cold at night,
Suffering and scared, people may be in fright,
Will this ever stop?
In the end the world will go *pop!*

Liam Tuck (15) & Abdul Kalam (14)
The Duston School, Northampton

Our World Is Changing

Have you noticed these things are changing?
The sun shining, climate changing, being homeless,
Animals dying, pollution's around, rainforests are cut down,
People at war, no food, no water, no money either.

There are good times, sad times, angry times, helpless moments,
This world is changing, we need some help,
Use a bin, to see us past,
Just think, it could all be a better place.

Becky French-Wade (15)
The Duston School, Northampton

Climate Change

Think in your brain
Of climate change,
Gases destroying the Earth,
When animals are dying from birth.

Trees, plants dying without water,
It's not much later,
Heat is becoming too hot,
No grass to spot.

Snow is becoming too thick,
Soon it will stick,
Lions, tigers going to freeze,
They much prefer the breeze.

Think of your brain,
Of climate change.

Perry Burford (12)
The Duston School, Northampton

Homeless People

Walking down busy town streets
Seeing people homeless and which don't eat
Wrapped in a blanket all curled up
Beside them a hat or a cup
Begging for money and even love
The night draws in and he finds a glove
The stars come out and the moon shines bright
Can nobody notice this awful sight?
Picks up his stuff and walks away
Think, this continues every day.

Rosie Worster (15)
The Duston School, Northampton

Do Something About It

There is so much poverty,
Something needs to be done,
Children in Africa are dying,
While we're having fun
Because they have no money,
Or clean water to drink,
We are really very lucky,
Don't you think?

Emily Liddle (15)
The Duston School, Northampton

Fears For My Future

You see me lying isolated, needles in my skin,
I see my future self, a rotting carcass in the bin,
My eyes are red, my skin is burning,
To be free is my painful yearning.

They dribble liquids into my eyes, not caring for my sight,
All I see is them, their faces, looks of spite,
I feel pain gashing through my flesh, as my heart beats
                                        unbearably fast,
And I feel vomit well in my throat as the fearful seconds pass.

This virus you call *AIDS* attacks our perished bones,
This is where we live to die, a claustrophobic cage, our home,
We spasm in our sleep, as dreams of death race through our heads,
And I'm thinking, *could tomorrow be my cruel deathbed*?

Holly Smith & Katie Thomas (12)
The Meden School & Technology College, Warsop

Going Green

The pollution in our world today,
Needs to stop, is what I'm trying to say.
Rubbish needs to go in the bin,
Green, brown and blue it isn't hard to fit it in.

Recycling is important; to you it might not be,
But it is affecting everyone, even you and me.
TVs left on standby, light bulbs left switched on,
All this wasted energy, will cost a bomb.

Using your car for long journeys is OK,
But if it's not necessary I've got something to say.
Walking or public transport, that is the way to go,
This will help to keep our carbon footprint low.

Rebecca Fretwell (12)
The Meden School & Technology College, Warsop

Being Green A Rough Guide

On the news and radio too,
Being green they're telling you,
Use less of this, more of that,
Eco should have been a degree we sat.

Use the bus, take the train,
To me it's just an absolute pain,
CO_2 why's it bad?
It could make a grown man sad.

So today I'm taking the bike,
Whether or not I may like.

Matthew Simpson (12)
The Meden School & Technology College, Warsop

Factory Farming

We all know it's bad,
We all know it's wrong,
So why do it all day long?
The animals are lonely,
The animals are sad,
I think it's bad, bad, bad!

Chickens can't move,
Hens can't cluck,
Pigs can't roll around in their own muck,
Monkeys are used
To test products today.
When it stops I'll shout 'hooray'.

But for the animals there's one last call,
Death will kill them one and all,
So for the animals the pain has gone,
But the scientists will find another one,
Will it stop? No one knows,
But for each animal that dies and goes . . .

They will have lived a horrible life,
Probably cried and cried at night,
They will have tried to break through,
Oh how I wish I could sue,
So what does this old thing hold?
Probably lots of mould.

Leigh Hearnshaw (12)
The Meden School & Technology College, Warsop

Poem In Trenches

Long-lost grounds,
Miles of open plains.

2 trenches,
200 yards apart,

Thousands dead,
More injured.

Officers shout the dreaded order,
'Go! Go!'

Over the top,
One man stays behind, knock-kneed,
He is shot for cowardice.

Running slowly,
Bent double with fatigue,
Marching to their deaths.

Poisonous gas spreads over the land,
Gas masks on,
Some too slow.

Still as a tree,
Staring at bodies,
Men crying,
Crawling,
Screaming for their wives.

Across the plains,
Poisoned with sadness,
Seeing my friend lying on the ground.

It's not fair!
Why should they die
For a country that lied?

Troy Davies (13)
The Meden School & Technology College, Warsop

Help Me Save The World

The world can be a better place
It's up to me and you!
You might feel helpless in every way
But there's lots that we can do!

Recycling is an easy way
So recycle a can or two.
Don't throw rubbish on the floor.
Don't act like we live in a zoo.

Being eco-friendly is easy,
Easy as 1, 2, 3!
We can all save the world,
You know it's not just me!

So come and save the world with me,
Save a can and you will see
A greener world for you and me!

Kiya Taylor (12)
The National School, Hucknall

Global Warming

Global warming, greenhouse gases,
All affect the planet's masses.
Turn off that TV, turn off that light,
Let's do more to win the fight
To save planet Earth!
Recycle cardboard boxes, paper too,
If we all do this it might save me and you.
So please everyone from every corner of the world,
Help us go greener and tackle global warming sooner!

Holly Wass (12)
The National School, Hucknall

The World Is Changing!

The world will be a better place
If you just recycle in a stage,
If you have a green bin
Use it with pleasure,
This is a key for better weather!

Believe in yourself,
This is the key
To a better place for infinity,
Pollution is damage,
If you agree!
This is a necessity to challenge, you and me.

Please recycle this can be a start,
If you have a better heart,
Remember this can have an impact on you and me!

So please recycle,
This is the key
To a better place for infinity . . .

Remember to recycle for the love of God,
This will help people to realise
Animals will be free!
They'll be like you and me,
If you help me, I'll help you!

Remember to believe in yourself!
This is the key
To a better infinity!
Just believe in yourself that is the key!
Save the planet to help
You and me!

Leah Newton (12)
The National School, Hucknall

Let's Stop This Big Mess!

Pollution is a terrible thing,
Which crowds the city with smog.
It fills the air with a vile smell
Like a huge hot blanket.

Cars and factories add to the mess,
So take the bus, bike or walk.
Without factories, where would we be?
But do they need to cause all this trouble?

There are lots of things you can do,
To do your bit with helping.
Turn off that light, switch off that engine,
Recycle that can, use your green bin.
All in all there are many things
Which *you* can do to help!

Craig Thomas (12)
The National School, Hucknall

Pollution Strikes The Forest

The rain falls down the forest,
The snakes slither and slide,
Water glides down the lakes,
The noise it makes is like a dolphin gliding down the sea,
Poppies and daisies flow with the wind,
The minds of the tigers run through the forest,
The rivers come to an end,
Pollution flows through the rivers and lakes,
Animals run as fast as they can,
The rain falls down the forest,
The lakes and rivers have gone,
The shiny sun shines down on an empty forest,
What are we doing to the world?

Holly Henderson (12)
Tuxford School, Tuxford

Poverty

P eople support one another
O ver seas, land and grass
V arious wars continuing
E very day of their lives
R eligion being the problem
T errorists making it worse
Y ou and I can prevent this from happening.

Nicole Meakin (13) & Bethany Rushby (12)
Tuxford School, Tuxford

Why?

Why can't people learn
Trees are not to burn?
Why do people hunt and kill?
Who would want that horrible thrill?
Why do people hate to love?
Why don't we look above?

Léa Gérard (12)
Tuxford School, Tuxford

War Is Hell

I look around, I see war,
Terrorists, guns and George Bush,
Tanks enter firing rockets,
Bombs are planted, guns are shot,
The USA start it off,
The army and the navy join in,
The airforce fires down now,
Their nuclear weapons kill,
It's all chaos, war is *hell!*

David Patton (13)
Tuxford School, Tuxford

Saving The Rainforest

Please help the rainforest,
Just let it be,
Don't cut the trees down or you will see
Anger, pain, sorrow and hurt.

Please help the rainforest,
Wait and see,
You can make a difference,
Come with me.

Please help the rainforest,
A difference we'll make,
Saving vegetation
For everyone's sake.

Kate Johnson (13)
Tuxford School, Tuxford

Our Earth . . . Our Responsibility

Whether we were intended
Or simply here by chance
Nature and fate decided
We should come into existence.

We were placed in a world of beauty
That provided us with a place to live
Humankind was fresh and good
We would share wealth and give.

Now Earth is a place of death
We have turned it into hell
Humankind needs to pull together
To make the planet well.

We are responsible for this world
We are its voice
We need to stop being so selfish
Just because we have a choice.

Tesni Hill (13)
Tuxford School, Tuxford

Reuse, Recycle

It's easy to recycle,
It's fun to recycle,
It's just one step at a time,
It won't take you long!

It's easy to recycle,
It's just placing paper and glass bottles in a bin,
It's just turning your heating down by 2°C,
It's just taking a shower not a bath!

It's easy to recycle,
It's just using energy saving light bulbs,
It's just taking old clothes to a charity shop,
It's just reusing plastic bags!

Vicki Storr (13)
Tuxford School, Tuxford

The Nightmare

Scattered carcasses of limp discarded change,
A mist of gloom engulfs the scenery.
What was once a lively inhabited land,
Is now as empty as a cloud in our hands.
All beautiful colours have faded away,
Letting our true colours come out from the grey.
No rustle in the trees of the refreshing breeze
Breathing life to all, standing in its way.
Screams and hate bleed out of this place,
The place I used to love.
The rainforest is like a faint dream,
Echoing into the darkness,
But the nightmare is just beginning.

Gabriella Irving (13)
Tuxford School, Tuxford

The Lost Soldier

There is no peace within a war,
All that's there is blood and gore,
Fear is seeping through every man,
No one knows the hidden plan,
War . . . war . . . war . . .

You don't want to stay at home,
You have to face it on your own.
Your country needs you,
You have to fight,
You need your courage
And all your might,
War . . . war . . . war . . .

One's down! One's down! You hear them cry
It's someone else's time to die
But your time will come I cannot lie.
It only takes one shot to die.
War . . . war . . . war . . .

A bullet whistles through the air,
It passes through your greasy hair.
You're falling, falling down a hole,
Not intact, a broken soul.
War . . . war . . . war . . .

Jamie Stevens (14)
Tuxford School, Tuxford

War

Why is there war raging today?
Can't we please keep the guns at bay?
Because the wars will waste our countries' bounties
When we could spend it on maintaining our counties.
One more thing you will agree on I'm sure,
Let us try to prevent war.

Harry Holden (12)
Tuxford School, Tuxford

In This Imperfect World

Words, insults, fly like bullets,
The fearful creatures run for safety,
But safety is impossible to uncover
In this imperfect world.

Cars hoot their horns incessantly,
People can't dodge the harmful gases
But any changes they could make are ignored
In this imperfect world.

Slumped in shop doorways
Passers-by totally oblivious,
The thousands must freeze
In this imperfect world.

Many feel powerless to simply
Change the ways of our unearthly habits,
Yet thankfully we have a choice
In this imperfect world.

Lauren Moore (16)
Tuxford School, Tuxford

Pollution

Pollution, pollution
There's never been an easy solution.
The air is full of contaminated waste,
It's just ruining the world's taste.

Pollution, pollution
There's never been an easy solution.
Carbon emissions that we produce
Are making the lives of polar bears reduce.

Pollution, pollution
There's never been an easy solution.
Typhoons, hurricanes, wind storms,
These are just some of the things that are killing people
As our planet warms.

Pollution, pollution
There is an easy solution.
By reducing carbon emissions and planting more plants and trees.
Those people who are ruining our world should be made
To pay the fees.

Laura Crosby (13)
Tuxford School, Tuxford

The Song Of Flooded Water

Where do I go?
There's nowhere to go,
Where do I flow?
There's nowhere to flow,
Where do I run?
There's nowhere to run,
Where do I go?

All entries blocked,
No hills to flow down,
Just smooth paths all around,
As I get higher
I carry things along,
Smashing and crashing,
Where do I run?

I carry boats,
I carry people,
I carry all their belongings,
I still get higher,
Higher and higher,
Where do I run?

Where do I go?
There's nowhere to go,
Where do I flow?
There's nowhere to flow,
Where do I run?
There's nowhere to run,
Where do I go?

Beth Robinson (14)
Tuxford School, Tuxford

Our World

We chop down the rainforests
And leave men and women homeless.

We cause so much pollution
And send animals into extinction.

But we also make so much litter
When in fact putting it in the bin to be recycled
Would be a lot less bitter.

We also cause so much war
And place people in poverty.

We cause so much climate change
Leaving people freezing or melting.

And we send people to foreign places
Causing people to be affected by racism.

All these points are to do with the environment
So stop them now and become eco-friendly
And be a big green eco machine.

So how about recycling paper, card and plastic
Or using energy-saving bulbs?
Or saving on your heating and using cheaper wood?
Car sharing and saving petrol
Name calling and thinking twice.

By doing this you make our future brighter
And by working together we can save
Our world!

Emily Blount (13)
Tuxford School, Tuxford

Nowhere To Go

No nice warm shelter
For me to call my own home,
I am never safe.

Dirty streets are mine,
The place that I call my home,
I am always cold.

Please help me be warm
And have a nice, clean, warm bath,
Help me find a home.

I am only ten
And I have nowhere to go,
Please help me today.

Nicola Stacey (14)
Tuxford School, Tuxford

Let's Stop War!

Bang, bang war is bad.
Bang, bang it took my dad.
Bang, bang it's horrible out there.
Bang, bang who? What? When and where?
Bang, bang do we need to fight?
Bang, bang let's all go to sleep tonight?
Bang, bang is it over yet?
Bang, bang if not we'll be in debt.
Bang, bang don't make that gun.
Bang, bang just start to run.
Bang, bang please knock on that door.
Bang, bang don't go out to war.

Maxwell Spurr (13)
Tuxford School, Tuxford

The Litter War

Litter is bad
Very, very bad
When we defeat it
We will be very, very glad

Don't drop litter, don't be square
Go and put it in that bin over there
Keep it tidy, keep it clean
Keep our land beautiful and green

If people don't care
And apathy sets in
Don't be like that put your litter in a bin

Let's win this war
The big litter war
Keep the world tidy
And the planet smiley.

Nick Cary (12)
Tuxford School, Tuxford

Just Leave Me Be!

All they do is talk,
Talk about me,
About how I'm so different,
Why can't they just see

That I'm just like them?
We are all the same,
But still they carry on
Calling me all those harsh names.

So why do they talk?
And why about me?
About how I'm so different,
Just leave me be!

Chloë Mallatratt (12)
Tuxford School, Tuxford

The Poor Little Baby Boy

Left alone, on the street
Like an abandoned toy,
Shivering and frightened
The poor little baby boy.

A life of terror and trouble to come,
He opens his innocent eyes,
Looks around the dirty town,
He lets out an almighty cry.

He has nothing to eat,
Yet he's surrounded by food,
He closes his eyes
And grey is the mood.

Bloodstained tears and mucky hands,
He lies on the morn,
His wish of freedom, to come true,
The poor little baby boy dead in the dawn.

Charlotte Callingham (14)
Tuxford School, Tuxford

Africa's Hope

In poverty hope is always there,
In war and droughts hope is spared,
In all children of illness, hunger and pain,
Hope can be seen in their veins.
Hope runs through all Africans' blood,
In every war and in all pain at every downfall
And in months without rain.
Hope cannot be seen, heard or smelt,
But it is always there, in an African's blood.

Abigail Harness (13)
Tuxford School, Tuxford

There Was A Time

There was a time
When I was big and green,
Now I'm half the size
Destroyed by a machine.

The animals that once lived here,
No longer have a home,
The people ruined it,
Leaving my children to roam.

Being a forest,
I just wanted to relax,
But there's nothing I can do
When I see the woodcutter with his axe.

He cuts me down,
Another life ends,
There was a time
When trees were friends.

Alice Weaver (14)
Tuxford School, Tuxford

Concrete Forest

Forest of concrete sandstone,
Grand old tree in the middle.
Humans, the tiny ants in the undergrowth,
Water running down the main street,
The main river,
Taking the ants downstream,
Taking them out into the endless ocean that is the world,
Which leads to many,
Forests of concrete sandstone.

Daniel O'Gallagher (13)
Tuxford School, Tuxford

Eco-Kid

They call me the eco-kid,
With my recycling bid,
Paper and cardboard,
An obsession to hoard,
Big red sticker on the dustbin lid.

The sticker says 'No glass,
On freshly cut grass,
There's a recycling centre
On the borders of Kent,
Recycling is no farce'!

Signs all over town,
'No wind turbines allowed
Damages the birds'.
Are there terrible words,
But if no new energy is found . . .

How will we survive?
I am the eco-kid.

Josephine Houghton (16)
Tuxford School, Tuxford

Reduce, Reuse, Recycle

The Brazilian rainforests are being cut down,
You can save them in your own town.
You don't have to pay for the litter,
Don't be bitter and not help us,
Please recycle and save everything from the end
And then you will not go around the bend.
There is no price for recycling litter,
Poverty is in the litter,
Reduce, reuse, recycle.

Steven Ellis (14)
Tuxford School, Tuxford

The Final Countdown

Under the crawling blue carpet
In the shimmering depths of the ocean
Where flashes of colour spark
From darting fish, suspended in
The bright coral, content, carefree.

But the clear water blackens
Silt and sand cough up
Approaching like a rolling storm
A sudden panic, then all silence
As the boat creaks under its load.

The cool, safe cave, a shelter
From the whirling blitz of snow
Here there is peace, a silence comforting
Where a mother bear rests her paws
And playful cubs pounce in the gleaming white.

Droplets of water stir the muzzle
And a deep rumbling ends all play
As the bears gather together in worry
The ceiling comes down in a shower of glory
And cubs lie buried under their silver nursery.

All things start but nothing lasts
All things end, all too fast.

Rebecca Bull (16)
Tuxford School, Tuxford

Stand Up, Speak Up!

R ocks thrown at innocent children.
A gainst racism we stand.
C ould we all stand up, speak up?
I f only the racists were banned!
S o think of all the racist attacks, and their affects.
M y God, whatever will happen next?

Jack Lindley (13)
Tuxford School, Tuxford

Change!

One big place, little time,
But we can make a difference.
The TV, radio, newspapers,
We all know about it
And we can make a difference.

So many people wasting away,
Not knowing the consequences of their actions.
Show them what's really going on,
Help them make a difference.

Laura Chambler (14)
Tuxford School, Tuxford

Recycler (Help Mr Polar Bear)

R ainforests demolished,
E co-systems destroyed.
C limate change,
Y ou can make a difference.
C an you save the polar bears?
L itter everywhere.
E nvironments polluting the world.
R educe, reuse, recycle . . . please.

Alex Taylor (13)
Tuxford School, Tuxford

No More War

War now should be gone for good
It has been put under the hood
So now Talibans
Have killed our Sergeant Dan
We shall say stop for the common good.

Alex Buckberry (11)
Tuxford School, Tuxford

Racism - Colours Of Death

A darkened room, an upturned face,
She tiptoes in, all full of grace,
Her head held high, her beauty shines,
Until the warning bells start to chime,
A frightening punch hits her cheek,
She cowers on the floor timid and meek,
Breathing in the kicks and harsh replies,
She stays strong, her tears covering her eyes,
One last slap and they're all gone,
As she blackens out she hears a song,
Suddenly she can hear no more,
Her eyes can't shine, her tears can't pour,
An upturned room, a darkened face,
The coffin comes in, all full of grace,
Bullies killed her, an almighty sin,
All because of the colour of her skin.

Paige Stones (14)
Tuxford School, Tuxford

Just One Tree

The chirping of birds, vibrant in colour,
The song of the saw, showing its talent
And the forest is silent once again.
Darkness descends and the deed is done.

Only one more tree spiraling down.

The predators prowl, hungry and desperate,
But the silence has silenced the search,
Yet thousands of miles away the colour
Remains on the tree table, ignorance is served

And the last tree cascades, leaves fall.

Catherine Old (16)
Tuxford School, Tuxford

Oceans And Forests

Oceans are 70% of our world
Vast empty spaces between land and land
Countries work together
With money and goods in hand.

Forests, also take up a large space
And feed the world with oxygen
But after we've chopped them all down
What will we do then?

Cod, haddock, mackerel - fish of the sea,
Waiting, taunting, caught in nets,
Wishing for freedom to swim in the open
Without human worries, without human threats.

Oceans are 70% of our world
Vast empty spaces between land and land
Countries work together
With money and goods in hand.

Mollie Knight (14)
Tuxford School, Tuxford

Earthquake In China

The earthquake in China was very, very bad,
It made many, many people very, very sad.
Hundreds, thousands are found dead,
A lot of them are found with a head.

The earthquake in China was very, very bad,
It made many, many people very, very sad.
Houses buried under tonnes of mud,
Earthquakes come with a terrible thud.

Jake Webb (14)
Tuxford School, Tuxford

Change The World!

You folks, don't put the rubbish in the bin
Put it in the compost recycling thing
Save the world, don't let it die
Or all the babies go cry, cry, cry
You gotta recycle, it's for the best
Wake up everyone, don't make a mess!
The ozone layer's burnin' down
Now the world is going down.

No longer will the tigers go roar
No longer, no, no more
We'll never hear the dodos cry
We'll never again see them fly
The endangered pandas are writing their will
Cos the mean people are wanting to kill!

Make the world a better place
Then we'll all be extra safe!

Kayleigh Dhiri & Guery Galantzeva
Tuxford School, Tuxford

Prejudice

P eople all across the world
R eliving the same horrible nightmare
E very day, just another struggle
J ust the cry of a victim's need for care
U nite across the world today
D ecide the fate of those who lay
I n fear, scared of the jeers that await them
C an you do something? I hear myself ask
E ven that, is not a question, but a trouble and a task.

Liam Booth (14)
Tuxford School, Tuxford

Am I Different?

You stand and laugh
    because I look different.
You told me to get a bath
    because my skin is different.
You leave me out
    because I'm not the same.
You kick me about
    because I don't play your game.
Look inside, look at yourself
    and you will see
we're not so different you and me.

Victoria Newman (14)
Tuxford School, Tuxford

What Are We Fighting For?

Hand guns
Big machines
Painful shouts and frightened screams

Planes are coming
Sirens sound
People shelter underground

Bombs are fired
Flames destroy
Father's workplace, baby's toys

People knocked
To the floor
What are we fighting for?

Hayley Stafford (13)
Tuxford School, Tuxford

The World Of Today

Where are the animals going?
Where have the rainforests gone?
People in the streets,
We've been hit by a bomb.

We kill all the animals,
We chop down old trees,
We make the world hell,
Please help us, please, please.

People are dying,
We're not doing anything,
We're not helping them,
We send help by a boat.

The cars and the factories
Creating all of the mess,
Can we not just put it right?
The world's not a game of chess.

We hide from the world
In underground shelters,
We should burn up the cars
In massive hot melters.

People are doing their best
But it's not working well.
All of us must try,
The Earth we can't sell.

Kieran Davies (12)
Tuxford School, Tuxford

War

War
War is poor
It should not take part
It breaks people's hearts
Some people die
And others cry
So please say bye
To poor war.

War
War is poor
Now stop
Stop all the fighting
It is quite scary
So please say bye
To poor war.

Harvey Marsh (13)
Tuxford School, Tuxford

The Cool Bin

There once was a bin
Who was in a spin,
He had a guitar
That played for Lemar,
He'd collect some rubbish
And have to punish
Those who did not collect the rubbish.

Declan Hursthouse (11)
Tuxford School, Tuxford

A Rubbish Poem!

Metal, glass, plastic and paper
Can take up many an acre.
Recycle your stuff,
Then we'll have enough
Metal, glass, plastic and paper.

Recycling would be a wish,
So help us all to accomplish
A planet that's green
And kept very clean,
Use the right bin for the right *rubbish!*

Jazz LaBanca (12)
Tuxford School, Tuxford

The Environment Poem

Cans, cans everywhere,
Bins, bins over there;
No one bothers to pick them up,
The bins are empty and have no muck.

This is causing one bad thing,
It could stop the birds from singing;
Just nothing is being done,
In this horrible pollution.

Cans, cans everywhere,
Tins, bins over there;
No one bothers to pick them up,
The bins are empty and have no muck.

Jack Beeby (12)
Tuxford School, Tuxford

War . . .

War is cold, brutal and bitter,
War is a waste, like unrecycled litter.
War creates poverty and makes you feel sad,
War creates racism to make you feel mad.
War is pollution to the rest of the world,
War destroys families on whom abuse is hurled.
War is not the reason for the climate changes state,
War is a reason why rainforests have a bad fate.
War should be a reason we learn from our mistakes,
War is the reason we must leave to give, not take.

Ben Knowles (12)
Tuxford School, Tuxford

Stop Pollution

Pollution, what a terrible thing,
Pollution makes the world sting.
For a solution to stop pollution,
Pollution needs to be minimised.
The people around the world
Should open their eyes.
Don't wait for it to get any worse;
The ozone is about to burst.

James Peter Webster (12)
Tuxford School, Tuxford

Recycle

Litter, litter on the floor,
Don't you think that it is really poor?
I think we should recycle to make the world a better place,
Hurry up and speed up the pace.

Litter, litter on the floor or in the bin,
At least recycle an old metal tin.
We want to play and have fun
So why are you sitting in the sun?

Get outside and help the world!
Recycle!

Louise Grewcock (12)
Tuxford School, Tuxford

Let's Unite

You are black and I am white,
You are short, I am tall.
You are thin, I am fat,
You are a boy, I am a girl,
You are happy, I am sad,
You speak English, I speak French.
You are unique, I am unique,
We are both unique,
So let us join hands and unite.

Phillipa Hardcastle (13)
Tuxford School, Tuxford

War!

Mars, Aries and all the others,
Smiled at their creation.
World War III has begun,
The world in its damnation.

Some think war is funny.
Some think it's a game,
Some think it's irresponsible,
I think war is lame.

The sound of guns firing,
The whistle of dropping bombs.
The soldiers shouting at each other
Over their radio comms'.

Poor Iraq, they peek out
To check that the coast
Is clear, but what's that?
The postman with the post.

It only takes seconds
To cut the postie down
And soon the family's smiles
Turn to tears and frowns.

This proves war is wrong,
Because innocent people die
And if I told you everyone lived,
Then that would be a lie.

James Daniel Barber (11)
Tuxford School, Tuxford

Young Writers Information

We hope you have enjoyed reading this book - and that you will continue to enjoy it in the coming years.

If you like reading and writing poetry drop us a line, or give us a call, and we'll send you a free information pack.

Alternatively if you would like to order further copies of this book or any of our other titles, then please give us a call or log onto our website at www.youngwriters.co.uk

**Young Writers Information
Remus House
Coltsfoot Drive
Peterborough
PE2 9JX**

(01733) 890066